Praise for No More Fear

"In the pages of *No More Fear*, Ashley Evans awakens believers to the fact that they are not meant to live under the menacing clouds of fear and doubt, weighed down by these oppressive forces. Fear is an inhibitor that robs us of our purpose and destiny. The love of God diametrically opposes fear and deflates the puffed-up powers of torment. Christ overcame the world so that we, too, might live devoid of limitations."

—BISHOP T. D. JAKES
Senior Pastor, The Potter's House, Dallas, TX

"In all the years I've know Ashley Evans as a friend and colleague, I have always found his passion, prayer commitment, and determination absolutely inspirational. He has pushed through many obstacles to reach and attain his God-given vision. Ashley is a true overcomer, and I know *No More Fear* will inspire people to never giving up on their God-given dreams. This book will bless and change your life."

—DANNY GUGLIELMUCCI
Senior Minister, Edge Church International (Australia)

"Ashley Evans is a spiritual warrior. He has fought and won significant battles in his life and ministry. The forty principles he shares in *No More Fear* have been personally discovered and applied in his life. This is not merely theory; it's a man's story."

—WAYNE ALCORD
Senior Pastor, City Church (Australia)

NO MORE FEAR

NO MORE FEAR

BREAK THE POWER
OF INTIMIDATION IN 40 DAYS

ASHLEY EVANS

www.InfluencesResources.com

No More Fear

Copyright © 2012 by Ashley Mark Evans

ALL RIGHTS RESERVED

Published by Influence Resources
1445 N. Boonville Ave., Springfield, Missouri, 65802

Published in association with The Quadrivium Group—Orlando, FL
info@TheQuadriviumGroup.com

Developmental Editing—Ben Stroup, BenStroup.com—Greenbrier, TN

Copyediting and Proofreading—KLOPublishing.com

Cover Design—Root Radius, LLC—Ackworth, GA

Interior Design and Typeset—Katherine Lloyd, The DESK

ISBN: 978-1-93669-998-8

First printing 2012

Printed in United States of America

CONTENTS

SECTION 1 — THE TRUTH ABOUT FEAR

SECTION 2 — THE TRUTH ABOUT AUTHORITY

SECTION 3 — THE TRUTH ABOUT GOD

SECTION 4 — THE PATH TO BREAKTHROUGH

FOREWORD

BY PASTOR BRIAN HOUSTON

Forty days is a significant period of time in the Bible.

In the days of Noah, the Great Flood continued for forty days and nights, resulting in mankind's rescue from extinction.

After Moses spent forty days in God's presence on Mount Sinai, he received the Ten Commandments.

Twelve spies were sent out to search out the Promised Land for forty days and come back with a report.

After forty days confronting and intimidating the armies of Israel, Goliath fell dead by the hand of a shepherd boy who later became Israel's most beloved king.

For forty days Elijah journeyed to the mount of God on a single meal fed to him by an angel.

For forty days Ezekiel lay on his left side and again on his right side as the iniquity of Israel was laid upon him and judgment determined.

After a three-day confinement in the belly of a great fish, Jonah entered Ninevah (what a sight he would have made!) crying out, "Forty days and Ninevah shall be overthrown!"

The Holy Spirit led Jesus into the wilderness to be tempted by Satan for forty days.

After His resurrection, Jesus remained on earth ministering the Kingdom of God for forty days before He ascended to Heaven . . .

No More Fear is a forty-day pathway of principles (or as Ashley says, "a prescription") on how to break the power of intimidation and fear over your life. Fear is a crippling emotion that works in direct opposition to faith. When we submit to fear, we are dangerously close to enemy territory.

God sent Jesus to deliver us from the tyranny of fear—once and for all—but just knowing this fact is not enough. There is a process whereby we learn how to confront our fears and walk free, through faith, into a life of promise and potential.

I am passionate about seeing people break free from the things that bind up their lives so they can live fearlessly in the pursuit of their dreams and their purpose. A key part of this process is to overcome fear—in whatever form it takes and from whichever source it comes. Fear from our past, and fear of what lies in the future.

Within the pages of this book, Ashley uses the platform of his own life experiences and journey with God, his struggles, the lessons learned, and the gold discovered to lead you on a journey through the intimidations of fear and into a place of freedom and abundant life without limits.

I have known Ashley Evans for many years. He has a rich family heritage and has emerged a strong and proven leader who is making a significant difference on the landscape of the world. I am honored to be included on this project and pray that you will walk away more in love with Jesus, more focused on the path that lies ahead, and more enabled to journey along it with NO MORE FEAR.

Brian Houston
Senior Pastor, Hillsong Church

NO MORE FEAR

INTRODUCTION

The ability to multiply is the secret to our survival. Growth is the basic building block of our bodies, relationships, business, and even church. When we stop growing, we die.

Families grow physically through reproduction and childbirth. Life becomes richer with deep, meaningful connections to other people. Businesses succeed when they create something new that meets a need in a different yet satisfying way. Churches expand as more people join together in a likeminded commitment to expand the kingdom through evangelism and missions.

But what happens when we stop multiplying? Families stop reproducing? Relationships grow stale? Businesses become more focused on managing their internal processes instead of focusing on the people they are trying to help? Churches turn inward and close the door to enlarging their territory of influence?

If our ability to multiply is the secret to our survival, then the greatest threat to our existence is not from our external world or circumstances, but from the way we respond to those circumstances internally. The greatest threat to our existence is when the ability for multiplication that lies within us is inhibited or, at the very least, resisted.

There are two lenses through which we can view the world. We can see the world around us as limited in its opportunity and resources, or we can see the world around us and the possibilities it presents as unlimited. The one who sees the world as limited agonizes over how to divide what they can see, taste, touch, and feel because the realm of possibility is confined only to human achievement. No consideration is given for divine intervention.

An alternative perspective is to see life as unlimited. When we see life as unlimited, we are not bound by what we can see today but by what we believe about tomorrow. If God is the source of all things and God is unlimited, then life, by its very substance, is not a known commodity but a treasure chest of dreams just waiting to become reality.

I experienced this in my own life. From an early age, I learned what it meant to work hard and, as a result, see amazing things take place from watching my parents and grandparents. Often those things were supernatural in nature, so I was aware of the contrast between the physical and spiritual dimensions of life at an early age.

It was during my teenage years when I first felt the call to full-time, vocational ministry. But it was years later, when I thought I was on top of the world and living out the calling God had placed on my life, that I hit a wall unexpectedly—and at the most inopportune time.

Maybe you've been there too. Sometimes we call this experience burnout.

I knew I had come to the end of my strength and was facing, perhaps for the first time in my life, a sense of limitation. I was scared, uncertain, and confused. Why me? Why now? And what on earth was I going to do about it? I'm a pastor. Were pastors supposed to experience this?

Just like you, I had a family who depended on me, a church who needed me, a staff of pastors who followed my lead, and a calling I had to reconcile with. Sometimes the loneliest places are in a crowd. But sometimes they're at the top. I felt helpless and didn't like it.

Jane, my wife, encouraged me to work this out through God's strength and not my own. I'm grateful to have her to do life and ministry with, but her words of wisdom didn't seem to offer much comfort.

I prayed. I meditated. I fasted. I read the Scriptures. That was all I knew to do.

It was in those moments that God sowed within me the truth that

He had a plan for my life, but the Enemy had a plan for it too. While God wanted to enlarge my dominion and authority, the Enemy wanted to destroy it.

Fear was the primary tool the Enemy wielded against me to cause me to back away and begin to believe the world was a limited place. He wanted me to settle for less than what God had planned for me. It began to cripple my ability to multiply and enlarge and backed me into a restricted space. Thankfully, I experienced a breakthrough and was released from the fear that had gripped my life. I was healed in a supernatural way, much more than what a clinical psychologist might scientifically deem a patient in recovery. I was empowered to face fear and intimidation head on, knowing that God's plan is one of unlimited freedom and blessing.

The good news is that God wants the same thing for you. Right now you may feel restricted by the fear of failure, rejection, and intimidation. I'm here to tell you that the Psalmist was right when he wrote, "weeping may remain for a night, but rejoicing comes in the morning" (Ps. 30:5b).

No More Fear is a book that has application for your life today. It is full of Scripture, but it is more than sermon. It is full of wisdom, but it is more than philosophy. It is a path to breakthrough, but it is not meant to be experienced alone. God will be with you every step of the way.

You will learn about the role fear plays in your life, how intimidation places artificial boundaries around your God-given influence, and how to live a life of victory, dominion, and authority.

Whatever strength, knowledge, or resolve you think you possess, it is the power of God working through you that will lead you to break the power of intimidation in your life. These pages are merely a prescription. God will supply the medicine and the healing you need to live fully free and experience the abundant life Jesus promised.

Are you ready to begin living a life without fear? Join me as we explore forty principles that will empower you to break free and accomplish the deepest hopes and dreams that God has already placed on your heart and prepared you to accomplish.

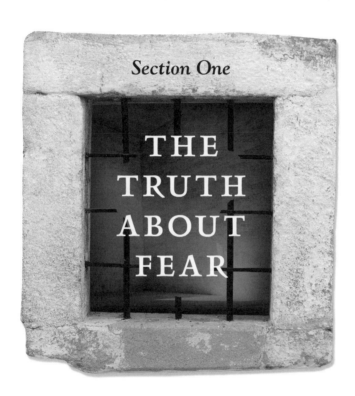

Section One

THE
TRUTH
ABOUT
FEAR

Day 1

FEAR IS NORMAL

My earliest memory of being afraid goes back to my childhood. We lived as missionaries in a remote part of Papua New Guinea in the 1960s.

Other than a nurse, we were the only Australian family living in an isolated area of Papua New Guinea, immersed completely in the indigenous culture. Although I knew no different, my childhood was not like the average person's, and looking back now there were many things about the culture that as a child I didn't understand and that quite simply scared me.

On the full moon each month, the locals would get together at night and chant incantations around a fire for hours, beating their drums. These "sing sings" frightened me so much that I couldn't sleep. I would wake my parents and try to convince them to allow me to sleep with them to get some comfort from the weird disconcerting screams and sounds that would penetrate the normally quiet nighttime hours. I used to dread these nights.

I also remember one day wandering along on a narrow jungle path, walls of foliage on either side, when a witch doctor in full garb, complete with a frightening mask, jumped out in front of me and started chanting an incantation over me. I was about four years old at the time and all I could think about was getting away.

Even more terrible was the experience I had when I was just a little older than this. One of the teenage boys from the village sexually abused me on several occasions. This caused deep a powerlessness and shame that gripped me, and it wasn't until years later that I was able to talk about this experience with anyone. Thank God He broke its intimidating and disempowering grip on my soul, but needless to say, for many years it left me afraid and unsure about myself. These experiences plus a number of others planted a seed of fear within me that would grow much larger as the years went on. It may seem simplistic to suggest that all my struggles with fear and intimidation could be traced back to these three events. Perhaps it's not that simple. Nonetheless, the fear and sense of intimidation that gripped me early in my life would return again and again.

We eventually had to leave Papua New Guinea about two years later because my mom became very sick. I remember flying back to Australia with my mom as she was obviously struggling for her life. When we landed in Brisbane, an ambulance met us on the tarmac, and she was rushed to the hospital for treatment.

I didn't know if I would ever see her again. It was a lot for any six-year-old boy to process. A sense of abandonment and aloneness only added to the fear that had gripped me when the medicine man jumped out in front of me in the jungle and the powerlessness that penetrated my heart when I was abused. It wouldn't be the last time I would experience intimidation and fear.

The truth is that fear, whatever its source has been, is a reality for many and has become an unwanted companion in their daily lives. It may have come in various ways, through both people and circumstances. Nonetheless, if we are human, we understand what it means to be afraid. Fear has its way of marking time in our minds and drawing us back again and again. Over time, we stop confronting our fears and instead expend our energy avoiding it.

Of course, fear isn't always a bad thing. Fear that keeps us from touching a hot stove, taking a curve too sharply, or falling off the roof is good because it alerts us to potential danger and offers us the chance to take precautionary measures.

But I'm not talking about the fear that keeps us from harm but, rather, the fear that prevents us from believing tomorrow holds something greater and brighter than what we have today. Fear that whispers that we don't deserve anything better, that nothing will change, and that the future is just more of what has happened in the past. This fear holds us captive and hides from us the truth that God wants to set us free.

Fear may be common to the human experience, but so is sin. Just because fear is normal doesn't mean it is from God. As sin separates us from a full relationship with God, fear keeps us from living a full and abundant life.

Fear is what keeps you saying no when everything within you wants to say yes.

Some of you know exactly what I'm talking about. This is the feeling you get every time you feel God calling to you do something that is beyond your imagination. Fear is what keeps you saying no when everything within you wants to say yes.

God never intended for fear to rule your life. The Garden of Eden was a perfect place. That means it was a place without fear. Can you imagine what life would be like without a daily sense of fear?

Your life isn't complete, and that means God still has big things in store for you. Yes! God Almighty has a personal plan for you! If you thought your life was doomed to be insignificant, marginal, or meaningless, you couldn't be more wrong about yourself and about God.

The Bible tells us that we are the salt and light of the world. What is significant about light and salt? Salt offers flavor and preserves what is good and meant for our nutrition. Salt prevents decay.

Light is also important. It dispels the darkness and allows you to see what is ahead. After a while, darkness can be discouraging, intimidating, and restricting. If you are experiencing darkness right now, you may be wondering when it will end. God does not want you to stumble around in the darkness of fear.

You can only be salt and light if you are living in the freedom a child of God has been promised. Imagine if you could find your way out of the grip of fear and be able to light the way for others to do the same! God needs you to add flavor and direct others to a way of living that is bigger than you might have first thought. He wants to use you to bring about supernatural transformation by accomplishing His perfect work in you. Fear ensures a dark, colorless, and tasteless world, but God wants to restore life back to His original design—one full of anticipation and adventure. And God wants to begin that good work in you today.

God wants to light your path so you can see what the next steps are and move forward with confidence and conviction.

God wants to light your path so you can see what the next steps are and move forward with confidence and conviction. How would your life change if you started living with confidence about God's call on your life, and with conviction that God wants to use you in an important way? It would change everything!

It's okay to experience fear—it's part of our humanity—but it's not okay to let that fear destroy God's plan to give you influence, authority, and dominion in this life so that He is glorified and His kingdom is advanced through you.

God has more planned for you than you've ever considered. God delivered Israel from Egypt through Moses who first refused to go to Pharaoh because he had a speech impediment. God chose to use Jeremiah to break his silence even though he thought he was too young. God used Gideon even though he thought he had nothing to contribute. In his own eyes he was the least important in his family and his family was the most insignificant in Israel. God affirmed and used David, even though his own father Jesse didn't. David himself had to overcome the intimidation of his older brothers and the warrior Goliath to step into his destiny. The point is that most of the great heroes in the Bible were confronted in some way or another with fear, and so will you. It's what they did *despite* their fear that made them heroes. What will you do with the fear that threatens you? Courage is not the absence of fear; it is simply what you do in the face of fear that assigns you courage. The question you must wrestle through is whether or not you will continue to allow fear to limit your openness to embrace God's plan to expand your influence and enlarge His kingdom.

Make a decision today to stop letting fear rule your life. Start believing God's promise that He wants to do abundantly more through you than you ever thought possible.

Day 2

— ·—·—· —

FEAR INVADES, PARALYZES, AND HOLDS YOU CAPTIVE

When my mother was rushed off to the hospital, my brother Russell, who was two at the time, and I were sent off to live with members of our extended family, who were strangers to me. Though they did their best, I felt abandoned and afraid. My parents weren't around, and I was in a foreign place with people I didn't know.

While Mom was being treated in the hospital, Dad went to find work. It was an unusual and uncomfortable situation. From the back blocks of Papua New Guinea and the familiarity of living and playing with indigenous children, plus the safety of Mom and Dad, I was thrust into a new environment of first world Australia, starting school and living with a family I didn't remember or know. And even though the separation only lasted months, it seemed forever to me as a six-year-old boy. The one place that was familiar to me was church. I knew what to expect and developed a deep sense of God's presence there. It was a place I could count on, and it was a place where I would invest mentally and spiritually.

Even though I grew up in what some people may think of as an exotic location, there were more fearful memories than good ones, and for a long time I didn't want to remember or talk about them. Looking back, it makes me smile (and my kids laugh) to know I didn't live in a home with a television until I was ten years old. So the idea of blending in with my new surroundings in Australia was a little more awkward than it might have been for others who were more acclimated to a modern, Western European culture.

School was an interesting experience altogether. There were three crowds: the drug crowd, the sports crowd, and the out crowd. I desperately wanted to fit in, just as everyone does, and found my connection through the avenue of sport. (Climbing coconut trees at a young age may have given me a bit of an advantage!)

Have you ever been in a situation where you felt like you were on the outside? Maybe it was your first day at a new school, starting a new job, or bringing home your first child from the hospital. There is an incredible amount of hesitation, anxiety, and anticipation surrounding these events. It's understandable, and any person would have these same feelings.

When you refuse to take risks and journey to places in your life that are different or unusual (therefore uncomfortable), it is precisely the moment when you allow fear to invade, paralyze, and hold you captive.

Everything new comes with a degree of risk and the reality of potential failure. Because failure is not celebrated in our culture, we rarely put ourselves in situations that force us to take true risks. We stay in jobs that we don't like because we'd rather deal with what we know. We avoid going back to school because we think we're not smart enough, too old, or don't have enough time or money. We don't try new things because we'd rather settle for what we know we're going to get.

When you refuse to take risks and journey to places in your life that are different or unusual (therefore uncomfortable), it is precisely the moment when you allow fear to invade, paralyze, and hold you captive. This is not part of God's plan and is not living out of God's strength. This is the path the Enemy desperately wants you to choose. It is the very reason many people are unhappy with how their lives have turned out.

We don't want to be the one to step out and do something new because we might fail. If we fail, then we might look foolish. And if we look foolish, we know we'll have to face the crowd of people who will say, "I told you so." Instead, we choose to stay where we are, enduring the agony of not accepting the influence, dominion, and authority God ordained and empowered us to exercise in our lives. In short, we miss living the life we've always wanted.

Being on the outside is exactly where Jesus is calling you to be. It is one of the things He told the people He spent the most time with while He was on earth. When you blend in with the culture to the point that the world can no longer distinguish your life from the lives of those who don't believe, you can bet that the Enemy is using fear and intimidation to hold you back from God's plan.

Just because you experience fear in your life doesn't mean you should abandon faith in yourself or God. When you abandon your faith, you rob yourself, your family, your friends, and your community of the salt and light God desires you to be. Christ-followers should live empowered, boldly stepping out and becoming instruments of change.

How would your life change if fear no longer held you back from following your heart, passions, and dreams? It would change big time. The good news is that God has already won the victory over fear and has set us free to live victoriously, not defeated.

The Bible says, "Now is the day of our salvation" (2 Cor. 6:2). The emphasis on the present moment is important. The Bible is not simply making a declarative statement about the facts of life. On the contrary, this one word—now—should empower you to do things and go places that you have never dared to go before. The prophet Isaiah writes, "Arise, shine, for your light has come, and the glory of the Lord rises upon you" (Isa. 60:1). That anointing is passed on to you through Christ and means you can be free from fear forever, if you choose to believe.

What is captivating you today? Are you scared of losing your job? Are you frightened you might not live up to other peoples' expectations? Are you suffering from a crippling sense of inferiority and wondering if life gets any easier? Are you suffering from loss? Are you struggling to be a great parent or spouse?

No matter what this world may thrust upon you, you should live with your head held high. God's children are not captive but have been set free. And that freedom was bought and paid for you by Jesus. You aren't limited to the circumstances and realities of this world. Rather, you should embrace the freedom and limitless nature of a God who wants to do exceedingly wonderful things in and through you.

Choose freedom, not captivity. It is yours for the taking.

Day 3

•⊸——⊸•

FEAR DISTRACTS YOU
FROM GOD'S PLAN

I've always thought the Genesis story about the Tower of Babel was misunderstood. Far too many people focus on the *what* instead of the *why*. In other words, it's often taught that the meaning of the story is no matter how hard we try, we can't reach God through our own plans and efforts. While this is true, I've always wondered if the motivation that drove them to attempt this architectural feat was grounded in some other desire.

I think the story is about something far more fundamental to our future and God's plan for our lives. The key point of the story is that their fear drives them to decide they don't want to be "scattered over the face of the whole earth" (Gen. 11:4b).It sounds reasonable Don't you think? Their motivation was to keep their community together, but it was a motivation rooted in fear. They were also motivated by the familiar. They were concerned about the unknown. Again, isn't this being human? If you've ever raised children, you know how much learning takes place in just the first few years of life. In these early years, children learn to eat, drink, roll, crawl, walk, run, and talk among other essential life skills. In fact, there is probably more concentrated development that takes place in our first twenty-four months of human life than in any other period of our existence.

We experience little to no hesitation during that period. Instead, we are open, we adapt, we grow, and we develop. Isn't it interesting how much more difficult change becomes the older we get? The dreams that seemed possible just a few years ago now seem out of reach.

The people in this Bible story are no different. God had them moving forward and onward. They were the descendants of Noah, the man who built an ark and, as a result of his fearless obedience, who along with his family was rescued from extinction. Life had been about as exciting as anyone might hope for. Perhaps they longed for a sense of stability that you and I might deem boring. Given all they had been through, boring seems like a pretty good option and stability was surely a lofty ideal to aim for. Wouldn't you agree?

This story marks the beginning of the struggle between God's desire for us to take risks and trust Him and our human nature, which avoids risks, struggles to trust, and looks to stay safe. The truth is that we tend to drift away from growth, risk, and change, especially as we get older. Youth has an openness to life that fades with time. The longer we live somewhere, hold a particular job, or identify with a particular crowd, the more difficult it is to begin to see ourselves living someplace new, changing careers, or gaining new friends.

Boil down all the reasons you might think as to why this is true and you end up with a raw sense of fear that distracts us from what our focus is supposed to be. In the Sermon on the Mount, Jesus said that we are to "seek first His kingdom" (Matt. 6:33). When we take our focus off of seeking His kingdom, we become distracted from the path that God has called us to walk and the life God desires for us.

What do you think it means to seek God's kingdom? If you are new to the language of faith, I can see how this idea might confuse you. It's not that God's kingdom is hidden, but that it needs to be explored, and embraced as our primary goal in life. It's a big concept, but it's not an impossible one to grasp. Think about the kingdom of God in this way: God wants to engage you in an adventure that is way bigger than yourself, it involves you breaking free, growing, learning so that you, in turn, can multiply what you have learned in others.

When you decide to pursue God's kingdom and all that it entails for your life, you will find yourself in the midst of places, circumstances, and opportunities that are beyond your wildest imagination. When you seek His kingdom, you pursue what God wants for you. When you strive for what you think you want or need, you experience frustration, lack of fulfillment, and general dissatisfaction toward life. When we are distracted, we can bet that fear is the culprit we must address.

In fact, something might be distracting you right now. Are you worried about debt? Are you desperately striving to get ahead in life, yet still falling behind? Are you looking to relationships to satisfy a deep need rather than center your life around a relationship with God? Maybe your marriage is failing or family relationships are strained and you are desperately trying to find solutions in your own strength. Maybe you are working with a singular focus on your career or education and have neglected to include or even ask God about His plans for your life. We have to identify what these distractions are before we can begin to realize the hold they have on our lives.

When you start to focus on other things, your desire is to stabilize. If the essence of life is grounded in our ability to multiply, then change should be a constant factor in your life. In reality, the pursuit of stability is in direct conflict with a life that is open to change. You can't pursue both.

God's plan will always lead you to the place fear is trying to distract you from recognizing, because it is the source of God's blessing.

You must decide what you value more: your stability or your obedience to the call of God on your life. The lie the Enemy wants you to believe is that focusing on your need for stability, comfort, security, and predictability is the perfect path to avoid risk and eliminate fear. Nothing could be farther from the truth.

Fear and risk exist regardless of whether we pursue stability or whether we are open to God's direction in our lives. In fact, the Bible tells us the only thing that doesn't change is God. Fear takes our focus off of building God's kingdom and places our focus on our needs. When this happens, we begin to see life as limited in resources, time, and opportunity. This is a dangerous slippery slope to attempt to balance. We will eventually lose the battle when we depend on our own strength.

Are we eager to watch movies about people who chose to do the safe thing? Do we read books or love characters that opt out of attempting anything that comes with the possibility of failure? Of course not! We watch the movies and read the books about and from the people who inspire us. Those are the very stories we cherish and the ones that light up our souls. We connect with them because we want to be the ones who are bold enough and courageous enough to step out in faith, trusting that God has a plan for our lives and has given us a place of influence, dominion, and authority.

God's plan will always lead you to the place fear is trying to distract you from recognizing, because it is the source of God's blessing.

Day 4

·—·

FEAR IS THE SOURCE
OF YOUR DISCONTENT
AND COMPLAINING

One of my many roles as pastor is to preach. In a sense, I'm a professional communicator. People count on me to prepare a message that includes not only revelation but also illustration and application. The more I'm able to preach, the better I get at it. It's not any different from a runner who gets faster, a weight lifter who gets stronger, or a swimmer who becomes more efficient in his or her body movements the more they practice their skills. The same is true for pastors and preaching.

When I received an invitation to speak at an event where eighty thousand people would be present, I was ecstatic as anyone might imagine. It was—in a lot of ways—the realization of a dream that I'd had much earlier in life and the fulfillment of a prophecy that had been made over my life.

Now, my schedule is very busy just like yours, and this engagement was booked months in advance. I had plenty of time to relish in the idea of preaching to a stadium full of people. It excited me and scared me to death all at the same time. But I didn't think too hard about it because the event was months away.

The closer the opportunity got, the more nervous I became. I started doubting myself. I wondered what I would say and whether it would make an impact. I worried that what I had prepared was not insightful enough or clever enough. I wrestled with whether or not I was qualified to be part of the line-up that included some of the finest preachers in the world. What was I doing on this list? How did this happen? Someone must have made a mistake.

Most people are more comfortable with the dream than the reality. When the dream is a long way off, it's manageable. The future is the future. Today is today. As long as you can keep those things separate, you are safe.

The closer your dream comes to colliding with reality, the more powerful fear will become. It causes us to call into question our preparedness, our decision to say yes, and our commitment to follow through. The result is a discontentment that comes from the gap between dreams and reality. This is what we experience when we know our circumstances are less than what we believe is possible. Complaining is our outward expression of discontent.

When you shrink back from what you know God is calling you to do, you are prevented from experiencing the blessing and power of God wants to give you.

Have you ever considered that the source of your discontent and complaining may stem from the very fact that you fear your dreams might actually come true? What if you became the CEO of your own company? What if God called you to plant a new church? What if God called you to give all your money away?

When you shrink back from what you know God is calling you to do, you are prevented from experiencing the blessing and power of God wants to give you. Webster may have his own definition of discontent, but I have one too. Discontent means not believing that God can do what He said He wants to accomplish through you.

I promise you're not alone if you feel that way. I've known many successful people over the years and all of them have confessed to me that when they practice their craft, they have to fight the fear that works against them. Confronting fear and intimidation is not about eliminating it. Rather, confronting fear is about removing the artificial boundary it has placed on your life that is keeping you from living out the dreams God has placed on your heart.

When we give into our fear, we experience discontent. This is not God's plan. God did not save you so you could complain. God has a plan for your life and wants to do something big in and through you, if you'll let Him. But in order for us to experience the victory God has already ordained for us, we must not give into the fear that keeps us from living into the life God has prepared for us.

Let's do a little exercise. Take out a sheet of paper and write down all the things that make you unhappy about your life. Then, make a list of the things that you complain about the most. I bet that the root of each of those lists can be traced backed to hopes, plans, and dreams that you have yet to realize in your own life.

It's sad to watch people live lives that are much less than what God wants to give them because they refuse to confront the fear that separates their dreams from reality. Jesus said it only takes the faith of a small mustard seed to move mountains. That's such a small amount of faith, yet it sometimes seems impossible to get even that much faith.

Your fear, as expressed through discontent and complaining, is the mountain that is preventing you from living a life of authority, influence, and dominion. It's yours for the taking because the battle is won. Jesus already conquered all that inhibits you from living a life that is completely in tune with God's plan. But it is a gift you must receive.

How would your life change if you stopped complaining and recognized that your life has meaning, purpose, and significance? My guess is it would change a lot.

When my feet hit the stage to preach in front of more people than I had ever seen in one place, I was as nervous as a cat around water. But God empowered me and used me to accomplish His purposes. In reality, that was His plan from the beginning. He wants this for you too.

Don't allow your fear to produce discontentment in your life—look closely at your current pattern of complaining and ask God to help you overcome the fear at its source.

Day 5

·⚊·

FEAR KEEPS YOU FROM CONNECTING THE DOTS

I remember reading about a particular group of bears in Indonesia called Sun Bears. These animals had either been taken from their natural habitats early in life or born into a sterile environment for the purposes of conservation and preservation. These bears are rare and were discovered to be on the verge of extinction until an animal rights group stepped into help.

Part of conservation involves helping animals reacquaint themselves with the wild and with their natural habitats. The rehabilitation and reentry process often comes with more setbacks than progress, at times. What should have been natural to these bears wasn't exactly instinct yet. In fact, the mere thought of walking on grass scared them to death at the beginning. They looked like bears but acted like children being dropped off at school for the first time. Slow exposure to the wild and to their natural habitat helped these bears adjust before being fully released.

This is no different than the process we might have experienced growing up. We spent the first eighteen years of our lives under someone else's roof, getting ready to be on our own, make our own decisions, and take care of ourselves. Then the day came when we moved out and started life on our own.

Fear conditions you to accept less than what God desires for you.

This program has saved the Sun Bears from extinction, yet it's risky business too. There is both the opportunity for success and the possibility of failure. That is the paradox of life with which everyone must reconcile.

People are not much different. There is such a thing as adaptation and conditioning. It's what we experience when we follow an exercise routine. When we first begin, our tolerance isn't that great. Our heart rate shoots up with the least amount of physical activity. Gradually, our bodies adapt and become more efficient.

We create a new threshold as our fitness level increases. If we continue our routine, we will eventually have to increase the intensity of our workout or we will no longer progress in our fitness. We quickly forget—months into the process—what it felt like when we began. Running five miles suddenly seems easy, lifting one hundred pounds feels effortless, and swimming one mile is considered a warm-up.

The opposite is true too. When we stop exercising, put on a few pounds, and become more sedentary in our lifestyles, we establish a new baseline. It's easy to forget what being fit feels like and the benefits it brings to us.

In the same way, fear conditions you to accept less than what God desires for you. The longer we live, the more opportunity there is to adapt to living a life that is less than what we are capable of living. Thus, we end up accomplishing less and settling for "almost." Fear takes away our ability to believe that dreams really can come true.

There are many things that can introduce intimidation into your life. Here are just a few of them:

- People's words
- Abuse

- Rejection
- Past failure
- The size of the task
- The size of the obstacles in our way
- A lack of belief in our abilities
- Past experience
- Fear of success

You've probably experienced several of the items included in this list. In fact, you could probably add a few items of your own if you thought about it for a minute or two. At times, your attempt to avoid these things has kept you out of your natural habitat, if you will, so long that you've forgotten the freedom that comes with being who God designed you to be and doing the things God has called you to do.

When you were young you probably believed you could conquer the world. You dreamt about the possibilities and the chance to make it big. You were willing to take risks, disrupt the trend, and challenge what others thought was possible. It's hard to admit but you stopped believing in yourself along the way. Still, life happened. You got married, started having children, settled into your job, and adapted to your predictable routine.

Then something else happened along the way. You hit a low point. Maybe it was financial trouble. Maybe it was a difficult point in your marriage. Maybe it was getting passed over for a promotion you were counting on.

That negative experience opened the door for you to begin believing that you weren't good enough, smart enough, committed enough, or lucky enough to experience success and satisfaction. So you began to settle. You bought into the lie that this was as good as it gets. You stopped dreaming, planning, and hoping for things to get better. In other words, you gave up.

Some of you have burned up in the midst of your burnout and have forgotten that you are a child of God, and that your Heavenly Father wants to give you good things. The danger in this is that you stop believing that even your stumbles or your failures can become stepping-stones to your God-given positions of influence, dominion, and authority. In other words, you stop connecting the dots and believing that all things work together to accomplish God's plan.

Jane is a terrific cook. One of the things our boys loved growing up was her vegetable pie. However, if the boys had come along an hour before it was made, they would have been shocked and horrified to see all the vegetables lying on the preparation bench.

Fear robs you of seeing the big picture and directs your attention to the individual things that don't seem to be working right now.

Each vegetable was unpalatable on its own, but the secret to Jane's amazing pie was what she did with the main ingredients. She would take the vegetables, sauté them and other secret ingredients, mixing them together, and suddenly what was "terrible" on its own became a favorite dish of the family. Romans 8:28 says that God works all things together for our good. Each difficult and challenging moment in our lives—whether it's been abuse, rejection, or divorce, for example—may be horrible on its own, but the genius of God is to take all of those individual moments, add His grace, and start to work them together in such a way that the end result is amazing.

Fear robs you of seeing the big picture and directs your attention to the individual things that don't seem to be working right now. Freedom offers you the chance to see that success is not the absence of struggle, but perseverance in the midst of your struggle. How sad is it when you give up too early and never get to realize the joy and blessing God has in store for you?

Don't let fear keep you from connecting the dots between your most important dreams and ambitions and reality. God has big things in store for you.

Day 6

FEAR FOCUSES YOUR
ATTENTION ON OTHERS

Being the pastor of a mega-church has its advantages and disadvantages. Mega-churches in Australia aren't as prevalent as they are in the United States. There are only about a dozen or so, and I have the privilege of pastoring one of them.

When I talk to pastors, they always have this idea that bigger is better. Bigger is just bigger, in my opinion. To use an American term, everything is super-sized in a mega-church. That means the good and the bad. While the size of the congregation, staff, and budget may be larger, so is the pressure, complexity, and pace.

I remember growing up listening to some of the greatest preachers of my parents' generation and thinking to myself how anointed they were. They had the right words, the right cadence, and the right approach. Everything about them seemed perfect. I wondered, at times, if the rest of their lives were as perfect as what I saw and heard on the platform.

Now that I stand on the platform, I know the truth of the matter. Whatever level of perfection you might imagine a mega-church pastor to have is an illusion at best. While public speaking is now something I really enjoy, there are still things that try and intimidate me as a leader. I have to overcome the intimidation that wants to stop me from addressing a particular issue with a particular staff member. Sometimes it attempts to keep me from speaking God's Word with passion and conviction when I know someone in the congregation doesn't like my style.

Then there is the natural temptation to look at my peers and begin comparing my leadership style with theirs. What would they do if they were me? Are they doing it better? It's a vicious cycle that takes my attention away from the source of my power—God—and places it on the source of my fear—my perception of others and what I believe they think about me.

One of the things that athletes do is size up their opponents. It's part of the pre-game ritual. While teams warm up on the field, the players are sizing up their opponents to see if they live up to their reputations—albeit good or bad. But this activity isn't limited to athletes or pastors. If we're honest with ourselves, it's easy to look around and size other people up too.

How did they afford that house? Why can't I drive that car? What makes them more successful than me? I have more experience and a better education; why did they get the promotion instead of me?

It's natural for humans to do this. In fact, it's part of our primal—fight or flight—instinct. This behavior becomes toxic when it refocuses our attention from the source of life. In the end, fear and intimidation sucks the life right out of us. This is exactly what the Enemy wants it to do.

Fear takes our attention away from God and focuses it on others and ourselves. Remember the story of Cain and Abel in the Bible? Cain and Abel worked to have an offering to bring to God. For reasons not fully explained in Genesis, God accepts Abel's gift and rejects Cain's gift. Instead of addressing God, Cain focused his attention on Abel. He became so consumed with jealousy that he killed his brother. The only problem is that Abel had nothing to do with it. God was the One who accepted one offering and rejected the other, not Abel.

I wonder if we have been so focused on how God has blessed someone else, that we have allowed fear to convince us that God doesn't want to give us a similar blessing.

The story of the Woman with the issue of blood is a great example of this. In the story in Mark 5, Jairus comes to Jesus and pleads with Him to come and pray for his gravely ill daughter. Every second is precious. Every moment they delay, Jairus's daughter gets nearer to death. They are making slow but steady progress when suddenly the processions comes to a halt as Jesus asks, "Who touched my clothes?" I can imagine Jairus being so full of anxiety and thinking to himself, *Of course someone has touched you; it's been me pushing you to walk faster so my daughter won't die.* But Jesus is in no hurry and takes what seems to be forever to find out who had touched Him. At that moment I've no doubt that Jairus was filled with anxiety and worry. He knew every second counted, and yet it seemed as if Jesus didn't care.

I wonder if we have been so focused on how God has blessed someone else, that we have allowed fear to convince us that God doesn't want to give us a similar blessing.

Often on the way to touch your life, God seems to be slow, distracted, and uninterested. He seems to care about others more than He cares about you. Our brokenness makes us compare ourselves to others. Why is God blessing others and not blessing me right now? The truth is that God often stops to help someone else on His way to help us. Why? In order for you to be encouraged and your faith to be built up. Why not see God's blessing on someone else as proof that He wants to help you rather than proof that He doesn't? The story in Mark 5 ends well, because Jesus not only heals the woman with the issue of blood, but He does more than Jairus had ever thought possible. Jesus raises his daughter from the dead, convincing Jairus and all his friends that Jesus wasn't just a healer—He was indeed the son of God. God is doing more in your life than you can imagine, so trust Him today.

The most destructive power of fear is found in its subtle ability to redirect our attention from God to something else. Before you can realize God's blessing, you must stop competing with your brothers and sisters in Christ. Paul wrote to the Church at Ephesus, "There is one body and one Spirit—just as you were called to one hope when you were called—one Lord, one faith, one Baptism; one God and Father of all" (Eph. 4:4–6).

The purpose of fear and intimidation is to divide you personally and create division and dissension within the body of Christ. This renders our lives ineffective and the church impotent in its ability to facilitate opportunities for spiritual intervention and transformation. Fear also comes with regret and clouds our judgment. Cain's decision to kill his brother is a great example of this.

God created you to be you—quirks and all. He carefully planned your life and anointed it to play a vital role in the redemption of all humankind. You are an instrument of grace, a child of God, and heir to the kingdom. Jesus is the ultimate affirmation that God loves us.

You are someone special. You have unique gifts and talents. You were created with meaning, purpose, and intention. However, your obsession with the blessings of others is just another way fear prevents you from the freedom you have in Christ.

It's not about bigger and better. It's about letting go of what you should have never grabbed hold of in the first place. Letting go will free you to focus your attention on God, the source of your blessing, anointing, and power, so don't waste time and energy competing with others.

Day 7

FEAR INHIBITS YOUR ABILITY TO DO NEW THINGS

P arenting can be an intimidating task. My two older sons are both over six-feet-two-inches tall. The oldest, Mark, has a personality that is definitely Type A. He has learned that his size and sheer willpower can discourage people from challenging him. When he was a teenager, he would use it to his advantage.

For a period of time, he tried to use his physical size and sheer strength of personality to intimidate his mom. Jane is a gracious person, but her grace is also tempered with tough love.; She might give in, but she won't give in forever. He found this out one day when she finally had had enough. No matter what she said or whatever punishment she assigned, nothing seemed to make a difference. His rebellious teenage spirit was tough to break.

This is when we drew the line. His constant disregard for our rules and our authority was too much. We told him that if he didn't follow our rules, then he would have to find another place to live. I'm sure we're not the only parents to have ever said that, but we did resolve to follow through.

It was the only way we knew to get through to him.

Guess what? He broke curfew—again—and we reminded him of our agreement. We told him he had a day to pack up his bedroom and he couldn't come back for seven days. He was welcome to join us for dinner or drop by the house for a specific reason, but he would have to make arrangements in advance. We told him he was now considered a guest since he no longer lived in our house.

It was the most difficult thing we've ever had to do as parents. We felt the weight of this decision because of the fear in our hearts. We were scared of losing him, of offending him so deeply he wouldn't forgive us. However, we also knew that unless we broke through the intimidation he had come to count on as a means by which he would get what he wanted, he would continue to leverage that method with us and others, and then his brothers would too, and that would destroy our family. This was not God's plan for his life, nor the approach a believer should take. Power by means of intimidation is not authentic authority.

Fear keeps us from considering new approaches to our same problems.

There is a happy ending to the story. He did stay with friends of the family for those seven days. When he did move his stuff back in the house, he was a different person. Had we not taken a stand, we would have affirmed his destructive behavior rather than free him to see life differently.

Fear keeps us from considering new approaches to our same problems. Ever wonder why you can't seem to overcome those things in your life that are holding you back from living the life of your dreams? We keep doing the same things over and over again and expect something new to happen. Someone famous once made the claim that such an approach was the very definition of insanity.

We would rather struggle with an ongoing issue than seek to overcome it. Maybe we don't want it bad enough. Maybe the thought of life without our struggle or pain is unknown and scary to us. Maybe we have allowed fear to convince us there is no other way.

It's like buying a new car. We are convinced during the buying process that the car we have chosen is different from any other car on the road. The color, style, and model isn't something we've seen before. Now that we've found just the right combination, we allow ourselves to believe that we are the only person with that car.

Then we drive off the car lot and into the flow of traffic only to be passed by fourteen cars that look just like ours. Psychologists tell us that most people don't see things they aren't looking for. That's the reason we're able to convince ourselves that the house we picked out, the shoes we are wearing, or the car that we drive is different. But when we start looking for it, the item suddenly appears everywhere.

Perhaps the reason why you haven't been able to break through the habits and hang-ups that are holding you back is because fear has kept you from considering a different approach. When we are intimidated and captive, it's hard to see past the prison bars that are blocking us into a corner. We stop believing there is a way out.

The Bible tells us that the victory is ours for the taking. The battle for our lives has been won. We are free to live and be who we were created to be. The only thing that is holding us back is fear.

You're probably thinking to yourself that it can't be this easy. It can't be that simple. On the contrary, it can be and it is. When you create unnecessary complexity about your life, you are inhibited from seeing things in a new or different way.

God's desire is to bring abundance to your life in every area—abundance of circumstances, people, and experiences that will make you rich. That may not necessarily be measured in material possessions, but material things aren't excluded from that promise. What do you want your relationships to look like? What do you dream for your future?

Whatever is holding you back from seeing a new way out isn't as powerful as you might think. The Enemy wants you to believe that you are trapped and there is no way out. That is how he wears you down until you stop trying and striving. The only thing left for you to do is give up.

The good news is that even if you have given up on yourself, God is still cheering you on. He is patiently waiting with all the authority of heaven to restore you to your rightful place of authority, dominion, and influence. You don't have to stay locked up, bound up, or bought up forever. The bells of freedom are ringing, and they signal the end of your captivity.

Open your eyes to a new life. God has already made sure there is nothing standing in the way.

Day 8

FEAR VALUES PERFECTION OVER PROGRESS

It may be hard for you to imagine, but I was in a band for many years, traveling and playing in churches, huge concert halls, schools, and hotels. We traveled together for five years, spreading the gospel through music and preaching. It was an exciting time in my life.

We booked gigs months in advance. It was easy to book events. The hard part was the playing and, most definitely, the preaching. That may sound strange coming from a pastor, but I had an ongoing battle with intimidation and fear for many years when it came to public speaking.

When I had to preach, I would tense up, my throat would constrict, and I just felt awkward. It was anything but natural. Whatever I was able to prepare in private didn't translate onto the stage. I can only imagine what the people listening to me thought.

I learned to cope with this nagging fear, but I never seemed to be able to shake it. When it was time for the event to begin, my heart would already be racing, my palms would be sweaty, and I would be afraid that I would just go blank. I prayed that I would at least say something that sounded reasonably intelligent.

Jane would always give me feedback after the events. Partly because I asked her to, and partly because she wanted to try to help me overcome this fear that seemed to grip me every time I had to speak publically. I appreciate her companionship; it has made life that much sweeter.

She was well acquainted with my ability to preach, as well as my calling. In reality, Jane probably had more confidence in me at that point than I did in myself. I know she prayed for me along with the rest of the group every night.

One morning I was preparing to preach at a church in a country town called Mt. Gambier. For the first time ever, I didn't feel tense. It surprised me as much as it excited me. Usually I would be a difficult person to be around in the time before I spoke. We had two babies at that time and I would ask Jane to keep them away from me before I spoke so I could concentrate. But this morning was different and Jane noticed. I was relaxed and even engaged with her in conversation. That morning I preached as I had never preached before. I felt released and, more importantly, felt myself for the first time in the five years I had been speaking.

It was a supernatural experience. After the event, the lead singer of our band complimented me and said, "Ashley, that was the best you have ever preached. Normally you are really boring, but today you were different." Jane found me and asked me what I had done differently. She, along with the other band members, remarked how much better I had presented and sounded on stage.

Looking back, I realize now that the source of my fear was my desire to be perfect. To be perfect means to be without fault or blemish. Humankind is in constant pursuit of perfection. However noble this desire is, it brings with it the fear of not being perfect. I believe this fear is more powerful than what we might experience if we were, in fact, ever able to experience or achieve perfection. This fear may have come from a sense of never being able to measure up to your parents or other people's standards; they might not have been vocal about it, but you always felt that whatever you did just wasn't good enough. Alternatively, it could be just a part of your personality to strive for perfection. Maybe it's one of the ways you feel like you can gain control over your life.

The fear of not being perfect is what pushes us to try the latest and greatest beauty products, trendy diets, and get-rich-quick schemes. We have this idea of what perfect is in our minds, and we measure ourselves against it. The only problem with this approach is that perfection is an illusion, for it is not something we have the capacity to attain.

The Enemy uses the pursuit of perfection to distract us from the truth that God is the only perfect being. If we convince ourselves that we have the capacity to achieve perfection, then we don't need God. If we don't need God, then our inability to achieve perfection is our fault. Therefore, those who are not perfect are, by definition, bad, or at least not good enough.

Do you see the vicious cycle in that line of reasoning? It erodes the life out of us. The only way for us to achieve perfection is through Christ. God doesn't call us to be perfect because we don't have the ability to be perfect on our own. What God calls us to do is walk in confidence knowing that our lives are hidden with Christ (Col. 3:3).

John writes, "You, dear children, are from God and have overcome them, because the one who is in you is greater than the one who is in the world" (1 John 4:4). That means you are not held to the standard of perfection but to that of obedience. And God's call is not dependent upon your achievement of any human standard, but by your obedience to leave behind all the things of this world in pursuit of the things of God.

This is really, really good news. Don't miss this: As a child of God, you are already perfect. And God already loves you perfectly. You can stop trying to earn His favor, gain access to His throne, or convince Him to bless you. That work was completed in the death and resurrection of the Christ.

You can stop trying to earn His favor, gain access to His throne, or convince Him to bless you. That work was completed in the death and resurrection of the Christ.

You already have God's favor. You already have permission to enter the throne room of the Creator. You already are the subject of God's blessing.

You may not think that it is true. You may not feel like it is true. You may not believe it is true. But God is not restricted by what you try to impose on Him. He is God, and you are not.

Don't allow yourself to be held captive by the idea the Enemy has implanted in your mind that you're not enough. You are a child of God, and that is more than enough.

Perfection is not yours to attain. It never was. Any attempt is confusion from the Enemy who is trying to take you off course.

When you are free from the pressure to be perfect and find approval from the people of this world, you can begin to relish in the favor that God has for you.

You will stand up boldly.

You will speak out confidently.

You will move forward with a new certainty knowing that, "if God is for us, who will stand against us" (Rom. 8:31)?

Day 9

·⌐·

FEAR CONFUSES PROTECTING VALUES WITH PRESERVING WHAT IS FAMILIAR

A braham is one of the central figures in the Bible. God gave him a promise that his children would be as many as the stars in the sky. This was an unbelievable promise for a guy who was already well on in years when he received this news, and at that time he had no children at all. However, this promise was conditional on his willingness to do something few would have been open to even considering.

Before Abraham was called Abraham, his name was Abram. The Bible uses names changes, especially in the Old Testament, to signify a change in someone's life. Abram was called to do something that we might protest or resist. God asked him to leave his home to go somewhere He had yet to reveal (Gen. 12:1).

Maybe you've never stopped to think about what he was asked to do. Let's consider it for just a moment.

Abram certainly had family where he lived. He had grown up and knew the landscape well. He had friends, a thriving business, and a satisfying lifestyle. Abram probably had a favorite restaurant, coffee shop, and donut place that he visited frequently.

Abram never had to ask directions because he knew his way around town like the back of his hand. He was looking forward to spending the rest of his life in a place that had meaning, history, and significance to both him and his family. There was little about where he lived that was unfamiliar or unknown.

So when God called him to leave all that behind, there had to be something inside of him that paused for a second to consider the ramifications of what he was being asked to do. Maybe his mother protested. Perhaps his family tried to persuade him to stay. It is quite possible that the local religious figures cautioned him to be sure he had heard God correctly.

In spite of all the strings that held him close to home, Abram decided to leave behind all that was familiar, all that was comfortable, and all that he had ever known for something yet to be revealed. How absurd! How crazy! How careless! What was God thinking?

As the story of Abram—and soon to become Abraham—unfolds, we realize just how significant this decision was in the course of events for the children of Israel. So much of our faith rests on his decision to leave that it's hard to imagine what would have happened if Abram had refused God's invitation.

What if Abram had reconsidered and said no? What if he had passed on the option God had given him? How would things be different from Abram—and even us—if he had forfeited this divine opportunity? It's hard to say other than it would have altered the course of events in such a significant way that only God would know.

You won't experience true satisfaction in your life until you surrender to God-inspired vision.

I can't help but think that God is also calling you to leave behind the life you consider familiar to go to a place He has yet to reveal in full detail. It may or may not involve a physical change of location. What if God is calling you to do something bold, crazy, and maybe even absurd?

So many people I meet tell me they wish they had the courage I do to travel around the world and preach to various groups of people. I secretly chuckle inside knowing that I have to battle fear in my own life every time God asks me to leave behind what is familiar. They look at my life as sensational, and they think that God only calls a few people to do extraordinary things.

I disagree. I don't think it is God who limits extraordinary living. It is people who are unwilling to believe in God's power and accept His blessing. You won't experience true satisfaction in your life until you surrender to God-inspired vision.

The church is a supernatural fellowship of believers empowered to carry out Christ's earthly ministry until His return. If that is true, why are so many churches and believers living lives that fall short of the supernatural transformation promised at Pentecost? It is because we have refused to leave behind what is familiar. We have convinced ourselves that it is better to preserve what is familiar than to accept God's promise to do great and mighty things in and through us.

Our traditions, our families, our heritage, and our history are part of what makes us who we are. These are beautiful things that should be valued, treasured, and celebrated. But when they begin to place limits on the people we interact with and the places we are willing to go—figuratively or geographically—we unknowingly choose to leave God's blessings behind in favor of preserving what is familiar, comfortable, predictable, and safe.

I can assure you, there is nothing about God's plan that is safe. The only safe place is in the middle of God's will. That's what the Enemy wants to keep you from experiencing. When the fear swells in our lives, we give in and retreat into what is familiar.

If this is where you are right now, your heart is probably racing, your head is probably nodding, and your mouth is hanging open. If this describes what you fear the most, then God is calling you to leave behind anything and everything that might stand in the way of being obedient to Him. Know that when you start that journey, fear will always attempt to hold you back. You must not let that happen. God never moves through people who are not willing to leave it all behind.

For the last fifteen years God has put on my heart the United States of America. I don't know why, but I know He has. I have asked Him many times to take away this prompting, but it's just grown stronger. Since coming to Australia as a boy of six, I have lived in Adelaide all my life. It's a fantastic place, and I love living there. For the past two years, Adelaide has been voted by Australians as the best place to live. I have a great church called Influencers Church, with campuses in different cities and countries around the world. I have a staff of 150, and I am comfortable. Adding to this, I have had the opportunity to mentor some of the nation's top political and business leaders. It's a good life, but as I write this book, I am in the process of planting an Influencers campus from scratch in Atlanta, Georgia. It's a crazy idea. It seems foolhardy to conventional wisdom. But this is exactly what faith is all about. Being prepared to step out and do something that scares and exhilarates you at the same time. To trust God and lay it all on the line. I like what Winston Churchill once said: "History will be kind to me, for I intend to write it."

The Lord declared it this way Jeremiah 29:11–14: "For I know the plans I have for you . . . They are plans for good and not for disaster, to give you a future and a hope . . . I will end your captivity and restore your fortunes" (NLT).

What a great promise. It's time to exercise your faith. You are more than your traditions. You have a history that is waiting to be written. You have been promised an abundant life. God cares for you and wants to do supernatural things through you. What are you waiting for? Go!

Day 10

FEAR CAUSES YOU TO SETTLE FOR LESS THAN WHAT GOD WANTS FOR YOU

Words have always captivated my attention. I love the use of words. It might sound strange but I love watching television commercials. I love hearing speeches and how people communicate.

I love to read and I also enjoy writing. When I was in primary school, around the age of nine, I wrote a short novel about a time machine. For me it was an epic approximately fifteen pages in length. (This was years before Back to the Future.) Unfortunately, my teacher didn't think my English skills were all that strong. He did, however, share my interest in math and encouraged me to begin reading great German mathematical theorists.

I really wanted to become a novelist at the time, but this particular teacher told me that my skills were stronger in math than in writing. He discouraged me from pursuing the path of becoming a writer. It's unbelievable the impact our words can have on other people. Our ancillary comments may unintentionally direct someone to a place they never intended to go.

Three years later, Mrs. Hughes became my all-time favorite teacher. She encouraged me to write and produce a story for the class using a vintage video recorder. She had no idea at the time, but her encouragement reignited a fire and passion in me to communicate with words that continues to this day.

At the age of fifteen, I received a prophesy on my life that I would preach. The person who spoke that word of truth left the conversation just as fast as he entered it. I didn't know what to do with that message at the time, but it would later prove to be very accurate.

It was a year later when I was confronted with leaving behind sports to begin a journey toward the path this prophet had so clearly revealed me to twelve months prior. Sports had become the object of my obsession. I enjoyed the competitive atmosphere and excelled on the field. I was reluctant to leave behind something that had helped me fit in with a crowd of people that I liked and who liked me.

You don't have to work, strive, earn, or plead for His favor and blessing. You simply have to believe that God wants more for you than you ever thought possible.

But I couldn't shake the feeling that ministry may, in fact, be the path that God had called me to take. I prayed that if I was supposed to preach, then God would have to take away my killer competitive instinct and desire for sports. My attempts to ignore my impulse to play sports were unsuccessful. God was going to have to intervene.

He did, and I haven't looked back since. Don't get me wrong. I still enjoy watching a good game and God didn't take away my competitive spirit. I'm still okay at most sports I play, but I've never wondered what would have happened if I had chosen sports instead.

Just as God had a plan for me, He has something big in store for you! He has already taken great strides to make it possible for you to meet Him right where you are. You don't have to work, strive, earn, or plead for His favor and blessing. You simply have to believe that God wants more for you than you ever thought possible.

Fear causes us to settle. Most people are willing to try something new once. When it doesn't feel right, they give up and go back to whatever is ordinary for them. It doesn't have to be like that for you. God has given you power, dominion, and authority to rise above your circumstances and confront your fears.

In the coming pages of this book, you're going to read about the power that is yours to claim through your God-given authority. The truth is that God loves you just as you are and has a plan to help you break through whatever is holding you back. But before you read any further, I wonder if there is a lingering fear in your life you have been reluctant to name.

It may be something you have thought in your mind, but you have yet to say it out loud. There is something liberating about saying what you fear out loud. Go ahead and say it now. Whatever it is. Wherever you are. Just say it.

Now that you've said it, you have taken your first step toward the blessing God has in store for you. Speaking your fears out loud reminds you that the power fear has over you is limited. Words help you put your hands around the things in your life that grip you and prevent you from living the life God has planned for you.

I want you to do one more thing. Write it down. This is like one of those before-and-after-pictures that people take who plan to lose weight. It marks in time what is holding you back so that when you finally accept the freedom you rightfully have in your life as a child of God, you can remember what it was like to live as a slave to fear.

> *The only reason fear is holding you back from anything is because you have allowed it to unrightfully hold a place of authority in your life.*

Keep this word, phrase, sentence, or paragraph somewhere close so as you read through the rest of this book, you can recognize God's movement in your life. I've been praying for you. Jane has been praying for you. Thousands of people have been praying that you'll experience true freedom and the breakthrough you so desperately need in your life right now.

The Bible says, "For God has not given us a spirit of fear and timidity, but of power, love, and self-discipline (2 Tim. 1:7 NLT).

Freedom is not something you have to earn. It is not something that is only available to a few. Freedom has been sealed and given to you through

Jesus Christ. The only reason fear is holding you back from anything is because you have allowed it to unrightfully hold a place of authority in your life.

It's time to reject fear and accept the life God wants for you—a life of freedom, satisfaction, fulfillment, meaning, and purpose. This will be yours when you stop allowing fear to rule your life.

Are you ready to take the next step in the journey to no more fear? Let's go!

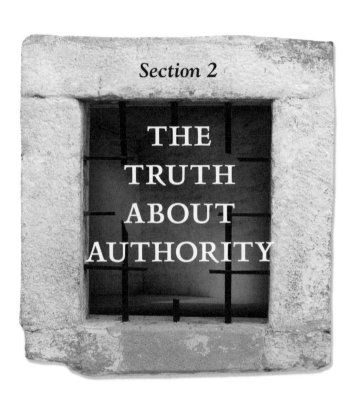

Section 2

THE
TRUTH
ABOUT
AUTHORITY

Day 11

—·——·—

AUTHORITY IS THE CATALYST FOR VICTORY OVER FEAR AND INTIMIDATION

Authority is a complicated subject, especially in a culture that wants both the ability to be free from authority while still exercising authority over others. Power, influence, and dominion are the necessary ingredients for change. Fear and intimidation are forces that inhibit our lives and reduce our authority. Authority gives us the ability to rise above whatever is holding us captive and dominate the circumstances that confront us. Authority is the battleground of your life. Whether you have dominion and success will depend on whether you grow or diminish in authority. The truth is that fear and intimidation are the stepping stones or tombstones of authority. How you deal with fear and intimidation will determine your authority, your influence and, ultimately, your success. What you need more than ever is authority. Authority gives you the ability to confront the powerful forces like fear in your life.

When a police officer steps into a busy roadway, what gives him the confidence to interrupt the flow of traffic? Authority. When a teacher administers a test, what gives her the ability to decide to pass or fail a student? Authority. When an emergency situation arises, what gives the doctor the ability to decide the method of treatment? Authority.

The recognition of authority, power, and influence almost universally comes from granting permission to someone to assign consequences to those who challenge the power of someone in a position of influence. If you are a dictator, the choice of consequences may be limitless—including death. If you are chief executive officer of a business, the choice of consequences may include firing or defunding a project. If you are a judge, the choice of consequences may include imprisonment—and maybe even capital punishment.

Authority, as it is understood within the context of society, offers a balance of shared risk and opportunity to ensure civility and social order. This is an important type of authority but not the authority I want to focus on in this next section. I'd like to come at this subject from an entirely different perspective.

There is much we can learn from the ideas surrounding permission and power. I'd like to borrow these words as we talk about the authority that serves as a catalyst for victory over fear and intimidation. With those two subjects so fresh on your mind from the previous section, I want you to know that authority is what gives you the ability to overcome anything or anyone holding you back from God's plan.

I believe that people allow themselves to be ruled by fear because it is more predictable than freedom.

God has given you permission to have authority over fear. This is so simple that we often miss it. That means you are only held captive to fear and intimidation when you choose not to accept your God-given authority.

If it's that simple, then why doesn't everyone exercise his or her God-given authority and overcome fear and intimidation? I believe that people allow themselves to be ruled by fear because it is more predictable than freedom.

Like it or not, we are creatures of habit. We have a favorite coffee drink, type of pizza, movie, book, and vacation spot. Something in our minds triggers a landslide of positive thoughts around those ordinary things that make them seem even more wonderful than they actually are. Perception is a powerful force.

This mind-power can also convince us that our lives aren't so bad after all—even though we are limited by fear and intimidation. We begin to believe that our desires are more about prosperity than about God. And we are wrong. Life begins and ends with our ability to multiply.

If your pursuit of more (whatever that may be) is inhibited in any way, then chances are good that fear has confused you and is trying to hold you back from the life you've always wanted. The only hope you have to break through whatever artificial boundaries exist in your life is to claim the authority you have in Christ. If you'll do that, you'll have permission to make mountains move and the power to follow through with such action. Authority will give you the permission and position necessary to act on the passions, hopes, and dreams that God has carefully entrusted to you.

God created Adam and Eve not only for companionship but also to rule over the entire earth, just as God rules over all creation. That same position of authority rests with you. The world is yours to manage and multiply in the places and people that God has given you the authority to influence and direct. Such power comes from the core of your being, the place where the Holy Spirit resides.

If you do not believe you have such authority over your own life, how will you ever exercise the necessary authority, dominion, and power to initiate the change God gifted you to bring about? I'm not trying to confuse you with words. I want you to understand that your unwillingness to claim the authority God has sealed within you at the moment of your creation, and which He released within you at the moment of your salvation, is the very reason fear and intimidation are wrecking your life—a life God carefully planned.

Authority is what the Enemy does not want you to understand or exercise. When we do exercise it, we place limits on the power of fear to hold us back from accomplishing God's plan. Breakthrough begins with the acknowledgement of the role fear plays in our lives and takes the next step when we claim the authority God has already prepared in our hearts for us to receive.

Just like salvation, it is a gift. You must choose to receive it. Authority is the catalyst to overcoming fear and intimidation so that you might become the divine catalyst God planned and purposed for you, the moment He breathed life into your nostrils—just as He did with Adam and Eve in the beginning.

Will you embrace the authority God wants to give you over fear and intimidation?

Day 12

. ⌒ .

AUTHORITY IS
THE PRIMARY BATTLEGROUND
OF YOUR LIFE

A sporting event involves three groups of people: professionals (i.e., players and coaches), fans, and referees. Each group has its own expectations, opinions, and experience that they bring to each game. However, only one of the three has any authority to influence the outcome of a game. Yes, it's the beloved (and sometimes hated) referee.

Referees have a thankless job. As long as everyone agrees with the call, no one really notices the referee. If a call is made that is controversial and impacts who won or lost, every fan, player, coach, and commentator takes notice and reacts.

Think about Jim Joyce, the umpire in American baseball who, in 2010, made a call that cost pitcher Armando Galarraga of the Detroit Tigers a perfect game. The entire baseball-loving world stopped for a moment in disbelief and wonder. Armando probably thought to himself, "What did he just do? How could this have happened?"

Jim may not have made the call he now wishes he had made, but his call resulted in the loss of Armando's chances of achieving a perfect game—at least that night anyway. Why? Because Jim was the referee and possessed the authority to do what he did.

Consider a similar situation during the Women's World Cup in the summer of 2011. It was Australian referee, Jacqui Melksham, who called for a penalty kick to be taken back. Among a multitude of controversial calls, one decision by one referee was attributed to helping the Americans squeak out a win over favored Brazil.

> **Authority is what allows you to push past whatever might try to hold you back and claim what is rightfully yours to possess.**

Referees hold ultimate power on the field where the game is played. What they say goes, and what they do must be accounted for. This is the reason why a referee who doesn't show or demonstrate a consistency in making good decisions during a game probably won't last very long in the profession. While there are steps available to challenge a referee's call, ultimately, the one officiating the game makes the call that stands.

If the authority exercised by referees can impact the outcome of a game, how much more can the authority of the children of God change the outcome of eternity? It can, and it does. Authority is what allows you to push past whatever might try to hold you back and claim what is rightfully yours to possess.

Whatever difficulty you might be enduring, whatever pain you might be experiencing, whatever stumbling blocks may be in your way, you need to know that God wants you to be victorious over it. Don't let fear and intimidation hold you down. You may have been used up, pressed down, and dried out, but God is not done with you. This is not the end of your story. It is just the beginning because every day is a new day that comes with a new set of blessings.

You are a child of God. You have been bought with a price. Your eternal fate has been sealed within the death and resurrection of our Lord and Savior Jesus Christ. It is not up for discussion. It is not to be negotiated.

It is not dependent upon you. Authority resides within you because God resides within you.

If you want to change your life, act on the authority you have been given. Reject the claim that you have been defeated. Defy the odds that are stacked against you. Become a symbol of hope for the world that God is still alive, moving, changing, and bringing His kingdom into existence through His children.

What is God calling you to do? If it doesn't make your heart race, your palms sweaty, and your blood pressure rise, you're not listening close enough. When God calls you, it will be to do something big. That means it will be larger than what you think is possible.

Until the thought of moving forward in the direction God is calling scares you to death, you will never experience the power and permission entrusted to you that only comes from the One who created all things. Jesus said, "I tell you the truth, anyone who has faith in me will do what I have been doing. He will do even greater things" (John 14:12).

When God calls, you can either choose to live captive to your fear, or break free from the restrictions of your present life and lay claim to the authority you have in Christ. Such authority has been given to you, but only those who step up and step out in faith can access it.

If you're missing a sense of power and confidence about life, you're not living in the power of the authority that is rightfully yours. If you're lacking the resolve to make the changes you know you need to make, you're not living in the power of the authority that is rightfully yours. If you're wishing you could overcome whatever is holding you back, you're not living in the power of the authority that is rightfully yours.

It is amazing how one person with authority can have a dramatic impact on decisions, outcomes, and resolutions when compared to one person without that same authority. The good news is that even though the Enemy wants to rob you of the authority in your life through fear and intimidation, he can't take it away. The battle is over. The victory has been won. Don't let the Enemy fool you into thinking the outcome has not yet been decided. That's why the writer to the Hebrews encourages us, "So do not throw away this confident trust in the Lord. Remember the great reward it brings you!" (10:35 NLT) It's our confidence in the authority God has given us as His children that brings the reward and enables us to carry out to the fullest all that God has planned and purposed for us. The Enemy knows that this confidence is ours; he can't take it but will try to intimidate us into throwing it away or laying it down.

God has won. The Enemy has lost. He might fight and it may not be pretty. But don't be confused or distracted. God has won, is winning, and will win. If God lives in you, then you have won, are winning, and will win too.

Start living your life with authority over fear and intimidation. Nothing can hold you back.

Day 13

AUTHORITY
IS WHAT THE ENEMY FEARS
MOST ABOUT YOU

Jane came home one day to a burglar in the house. If you've never had your home broken into, it is a frightening experience. To know that someone has been inside the one place you consider a refuge from the outside world is unnerving. To actually be in the home with them is surreal.

It has never crossed my mind to break into someone else's home, but I would imagine that it takes some guts. You're never really sure what you're going to find or what to expect. I guess, in a lot of ways, you just hope for the best. Perhaps this burglar wished he had broken into the house next door after what happened next.

Jane had just arrived home with our six-week-old son after dinner with her parents. When she walked in the door, she heard a noise coming from our laundry room. Being the spontaneous type of person she is, she called out my name and opened the door to the laundry room only to come face-to-face with a robber who was desperately trying to unlock the side door of the house and make his escape.

Jane was standing three feet from this guy who had a bag in his hand with some of our possessions. Instead of screaming or running like most people might have, Jane, with a baby in her arms, confronted the guy with a voice of forceful authority. "Who do you think you are and what are you doing in my house?" she said, as she looked him straight in the eye.

He didn't know what to say and mumbled a weak excuse. Jane replied, "Get out of my house." The robber shuffled by her and started to walk down the corridor when Jane noticed our screwdriver sticking out of his back pocket. Indignant that he would dare steal anything, especially, our two-dollar screwdriver, she yelled at him, "Hey, that's our screwdriver!" Jane proceeded to pull it out of his back pocket.

The guy—now feeling compelled to get out of the house as quickly as possible—walked down the hallway toward the front door with Jane following, brandishing the screwdriver. Just as he thought he might be safe, Jane's mother walked in the front door, took one look at the young man in his twenties, and then looked at Jane's face. Instantly, she stepped in front of him and asked with an aggressive tone, "And who are you?"

Then Jane's Dad walked in and made a citizen's arrest before the thief could make it out the door. He pushed the man to the ground and then sat on him while they waited for the police to arrive. I bet this guy never dreamed of such a series of encounters when he decided to break into our house that day. What might have been routine for him turned out to be anything but a routine experience.

Can you imagine what was going through this guy's mind? Perhaps he had hoped to find some precious jewels, maybe lift a TV or stereo. What we discovered later was that this robber had committed a string of armed robberies in the previous weeks and was wanted by the police.

This guy was a professional. But now he was lying on the ground, under citizen's arrest, and enduring the weight of my in-laws until the authorities arrived. All the while, my mother-in-law ministered to him. She told him he needed to accept Jesus into his heart and change his ways.

This burglar had planned on the fact that no one would be home. Had the course of events played out just as he had envisioned it in his mind, he never would have had to deal with confronting three separate individuals on his way out of the house. He would have stolen what he thought was valuable and moved on.

The surprise that Jane and her parents brought to the situation changed the priority of the people in the room. Before their arrival home, he was in complete control of the situation. He had come and would go as he had planned, even if it was our house.

When he realized he was no longer alone in the house, he knew a shift in power had taken place. No longer was he in charge or free to roam and rummage through our house. No longer did he have the time to linger. His only concern was getting out of the house and away from Jane and her parents.

What do we call this power that gives one person the right to be in their home and the other person the right to leave immediately? Authority. Without authority, the burglar had nothing to be afraid of. Since Jane had authority, this burglar had everything to be afraid of.

It is no different in our lives. The Enemy tries to infringe upon our authority by breaking through the weak points in our lives. Sometimes that is reminding us of past failures. Other times that comes in the form of perceived opposition to God's plan. He also tries to direct attention anywhere and everywhere that might make us forget or give up—even for a short period of time—the power and authority God has given to us.

The Bible says, "You, dear children, are from God and have overcome . . . because the one who is in you is greater than the one who is in the world" (1 John 4:4). This means that however the Enemy attempts to reduce the size of your influence or diminish your dominion over specific areas of your life, he is limited and will not stand the test of time. It is only when you yield power to the Enemy that is he given the ability and opportunity to employ fear and intimidation to keep you from exercising the authority that is yours to possess.

> *Whatever power, fear, and intimidation have played in your life, the power of your authority is greater.*

The Enemy knows he can't undermine your authority forever. He knows his power is limited and so is his right to roam freely through your life. His goal is to keep you distracted by focusing your attention on just about anything. He knows the longer you take to exert your authority, the more difficult it becomes.

Whatever power, fear, and intimidation have played in your life, the power of your authority is greater. However the Enemy has held you back, the power of your authority is greater. Whenever you feel overwhelmed, sad, or out of control, the power of your authority is greater.

The Enemy knows that when you accept the freedom you have in Christ, there is nothing he can do to stop you. He is hopelessly powerless in the face of the dominion, power, and authority God has given you.

One of the last things you did in the previous section was to call out loud the fears that were holding you back from the life God designed you to live. Did you know that the very second those words came out of your mouth, you started to limit the power the Enemy plays in your life? That one step initiated a domino effect that will lead you down the path to total freedom.

The great paradox is this: Whatever we fear is no match to the fear the Enemy feels when we exercise authority in our lives. Our perception of whatever we fear sometimes leads us to conclude that our fear is more powerful than it really is. Even so, the Enemy is working diligently to ensure you never discover what you are learning in this book.

A life liberated from fear is perhaps one of the most powerful forces for good our world will experience this side of heaven. This is what God wants for you and has made accessible to you today, right where you are. Don't let the Enemy confuse you any longer. Step into the authority that is rightfully yours.

Day 14

⟶

AUTHORITY HAS BEEN GIVEN TO YOU THROUGH CHRIST

The first time I met the then-prime minister of Australia was in a private meeting in his Canberra offices with his assistant and myself and two colleagues. I was meeting him on his terms and at the time he had allotted.

Already nervous, I was doing my best to stay calm and clear-headed. I didn't want to waste this important opportunity, so I had prepared a list of items that I wanted to discuss with him. I practiced talking through them several times in advance of the appointed day.

While waiting in the room, I tried to make small talk with others, but I was also rehearsing the list in my mind. If you've ever waited at a restaurant or anywhere for a meeting, you know how awkward and agonizing the wait can be. It is ten times worse when it's somebody in a significant position like the prime minister of a country.

I was just starting to relax when the prime minister's arrival was announced a few minutes in advance of his entering the room. My preparation kicked in and I felt ready for this opportunity. That is until he actually entered the room.

There was something that happened that I couldn't have foretold. It was like the air had been sucked out of the room. All the preparation and mind rehearsing couldn't have prepared me for this moment. Not only did the atmosphere change, so did the posture of everyone in the room.

The prime minister was just a guy like me. He had to sleep the night before because he was tired. He had to shower and eat breakfast that day, just like me. He had to get in a vehicle that took him from his house to where we were meeting, just like me. Only when he entered the room, he was nothing like me. He entered the room not as an ordinary man but as the prime minister of Australia. It was sensational.

I'm not a short guy, and he is. I've spent my life around people who hold a significant position. I was ready for this moment, or so I thought. My confidence level went out the window with my stomach. I may have been calm, cool, and collected in front of the mirror or with Jane, but I was a meek as a lamb in that moment.

Knowing that the prime minister was a human being—a man willing to meet with me—how did he transform into this larger-than-life figure that stole the air from the room? Simple. Authority. He holds a position that not only comes with a history of significant people but he has the ability to make important decisions that shape the lives and future of all who call themselves Australians.

As I reflect on that experience, I can't help but wonder what it must have been like to encounter Jesus. His reputation always preceded Him. Meeting Jesus must have felt like I did when I met the prime minister and more. The Bible records multiple accounts where Jesus is recognized as someone who has authority:

"They were amazed at his teaching, because his message had authority" (Luke 4:32).

"The people were all so amazed that they asked each other, 'What is this? A new teaching—and with authority'" (Mark 1:27).

"'But I want you to know that the Son of Man has authority on earth to forgive sins.' So he said to the paralyzed man, 'Get up, take your mat and go home.' Then the man got up and went home" (Matt. 9:6–7).

When Jesus spoke, things happened. Very often, those things involved a supernatural dimension of reality that accomplished things no one else thought was possible. Storms were calmed, demons obeyed, and people were healed. Why? Because Jesus had authority.

You, too, have been given authority.

"Jesus called his disciples to him and gave them authority to heal the sick" (Matt. 10:1).

"Then Jesus came to them and said, 'All authority in heaven and on earth has been given to me. Therefore go into all the world an preach the gospel'" (Matt. 26:18).

It's my prayer that you would understand the authority you have in Jesus. Once you do, everything in your life will change. Just as Adam had dominion and authority under God, you have authority under Jesus. Jesus died so you could reclaim the authority relinquished by Adam.

If you feel powerless, Christ will be powerful in you. If you feel defeated, Christ will be the victor through you. If you feel like giving up, Christ will be your strength.

Whatever obstacles you face, you are not alone. However difficult the road seems ahead, you don't have to rely on your own strength. Whenever you are reminded of that which you fear the most, you can rest in the authority of Christ that has no limits.

Whenever you are reminded of that which you fear the most, you can rest in the authority of Christ that has no limits.

The Christ who lives in you has already given you all the authority you'll need to overcome the fear holding you back from supernatural breakthrough. Keep reading!

Day 15

＊─＊

AUTHORITY SETS YOU
APART TO ACCOMPLISH
GREAT THINGS

I t never occurred to me that Politics, while an interesting subject, might be a place God would use me to influence others. When my Dad and I started a political party in Australia, no one rolled out the red carpet and welcomed us. We believed that the family needed a champion in a post-Christian culture that was glamorizing adultery, abuse, and narcissism. If left unchecked this would eventually lead to a complete implosion of human dignity and the integrity of our faith in God.

Family First was a chance to influence decision-making that affected everyday families. We were already talking about the importance of family in church. We were teaching parents about godly parenting. We were providing opportunities for children to grow in their knowledge of the things of God. But something within me was restless, and I knew there were other frontiers that could be taken.

Have you ever gotten up early in the morning with a sense that something big was about to happen? That happened to me four mornings in a row during February 2000. I woke up with a huge burden and an overwhelming sense that God was calling me to start a political party that would champion the family in a post-Christian culture.

The words I heard were, "You have ten years to make a difference, or your freedoms you take for granted will be gone forever." The call was strong and clear. I remember discussing it with Jane and several people on my pastoral team who were on a retreat with me at the time.

On the way home, I spoke to one of our staff about what the political party would stand for and how it would be a secular party that championed the voice of ordinary families. It wasn't going to be a church thing. I thought that might confuse the issue. It needed to be a stand-alone initiative that wasn't directly tied to any one church.

That night, my Dad called and wanted to talk about something on his mind over coffee. During our conversation, he said to me, "Ashley, a local politician [now a national senator] suggested I run for parliament. What do you think?" I couldn't believe what I was hearing, as I hadn't discussed with my dad what had happened on the retreat. We had never even had a conversation of this nature at any time in our lives.

I said, "Dad, stop. I've got to tell you what happened this week." That was the night my Dad and I decided to start Family First. Our party would go on to have four senators elected and hold the balance of power with one other senator in our Federal parliament for six years.

There were a lot of people who told me that I shouldn't get into politics. What business does a pastor have on the political scene? How would we raise the money? How would we get enough members to register our party? Where on earth would we get the candidates?

People thought we were crazy and presumptuous. Intimidation and fear tried to stop us. But as the pressure mounted, so did my excitement and my resolve. It just confirmed I was moving in the right direction.

I have to say that that experience was challenging. It was the most pressure I have ever experienced in my life. It would have been easy to quit and give up under the relentless pressure and intimidation, but we didn't quit. We pushed through and won. The nights of the elections in

2001 and 2004 were probably two of the most amazing highs in my entire life. We, along with the entire nation, watched as we won seats in the senate and became a voice for families. This influence helped stop a slew of pervasive measures that would have restricted long-held freedoms in our country.

The Enemy wants to wear you out and intimidate you until you give up. You've probably thought about giving up. Maybe you're tired. Maybe you feel like you can't do it. Intimidation will make you feel like no one cares and no one really wants to help. The promise of God is that you will never be alone.

If you've ever felt this way, you're not alone. Anyone who has ever accomplished anything of significance has felt like this. A life that acts with authority is not one that is absent of adversity. I have never met a leader, pastor, or person of influence who has not continued to experience fear and intimidation in their lives.

Yes, you have the victory in Christ. Yes, you have been given all authority, dominion, and power under heaven to accomplish whatever plans He has placed on your heart. Yes, you have been set apart for great things.

You can relish in those promises, but you must also know that with authority comes adversity. The fundamental problem I have with positive thinking alone is that it does not prepare you to exercise your God-given authority when adversity comes. The war for your soul may have been won, but there is a still a battle raging orchestrated to hold you back, distract you, and keep you from doing great things.

Authority is the piece of the puzzle the Enemy hopes you won't connect to the rest of your life. As long as he can keep you from discovering the empowerment that comes through God's authority, he knows you will be limited in becoming a difference maker in your community and culture. He is counting on you to back away when the cost of following through seems too great.

Remember, the Enemy is great at taking a truth and bending it into an almost truth. The cost of obedience will certainly be high, but the cost of disobedience is an ordinary life that is full of unfulfilled dreams and unmet expectations. This is not the life God wants for you. You are wasting time, opportunity, and resources when you take your eyes off the goal and allow your heart to become numb through the adversity you face.

Doing great things always comes with a sense that life is out of control. The reason you feel like this is because change happens in the midst of uncertainty and doubt. If we had a crystal ball and could see into the future, it would remove the faith required to bring about spiritual transformation in our lives and the lives God has given us authority to influence.

The reason you see your life as limited is because you have bought into the lie the Enemy had peddled to you.

When I say that living a life out of control is God's plan, I'm not referring to destructive habits. God's plan is not to destroy you like destructive habits often do. In fact, destructive habits are the result of fear and intimidation ruling our lives rather than a life that believes in the authority he or she has been given in Christ.

Authority gives you the ability to speak when others say no one will listen. It gives you the courage to act when others say it's not worth the price. It gives you the power to succeed when others say it will fail.

The reason you see your life as limited is because you have bought into the lie the Enemy had peddled to you. You don't think God really wants to use you. You don't believe you have the authority Jesus has given to you. You don't want it bad enough to push through the adversity so you can be liberated to do great things.

Freedom is yours, yet you choose captivity.

Fulfillment is yours, yet you choose to live conflicted.

Fantastic things are ahead of you, yet you choose to relive your past.

God wants to do things in and through you that are bigger, bolder, and more audacious than you ever dreamed. He has given you the measure of authority you need to do something of significance. The reason your life isn't what you want it to be is because you have a faith problem, not a resource problem. God will accomplish great things through you if you'll let Him. Whatever adversity you might face, you need to know you will prevail and go on to do great things.

Day 16

⋅—⋅

AUTHORITY GRANTS
YOU ACCESS TO PLACES
OTHERS CAN'T GO

B eing a pastor of one of only a few mega-churches in Australia gives me a solid platform to influence others. But there is a limit to what a pastor can do, especially in a post-Christian culture. There was a time in the history of the church when the pastor was held in great esteem, was welcomed by State officials, and was revered as a holy person. But not today. Today pastors are esteemed in their local church, but that is often where it stops. The church is no longer the centre of society; the shopping center is. Christianity is no longer the driving force for society; secularism is, especially in Western countries. The pervading lie championed by secularists and believed by most Christians is "the separation of church and state" It is quoted as being the cornerstone of a good society, but in reality its intended to intimidate Christians and keep them from being influencers for good in their world.

This attitude is what makes my move into politics a significant one.

As discussed, Family First began as a movement to challenge a barrage of decisions coming from our government that infringed upon the role of the family. Armed with an agenda, the government was slowly moving away from basing itself on any biblical definition of family. As a Christian I considered this an assault on my freedom of religion. As a husband and father, I feared what kind of Australia my kids would grow up in if things continued to move in the same direction.

Politics allowed me to step outside the platform of being a church pastor and move into a realm where we could address these misguided decisions directly. It would not be easy, but I was convinced this was the path we needed to take. I believed God had given me supernatural direction and authority to champion the family on the national political scene.

I knew that I could not be the face of the campaign. Part of that was lingering fear and insecurity, and part of that decision was pragmatic. I knew I could comment on the moral issues of society from the pulpit as a pastor. However, if I were to be part of the government, it might call into question my integrity and jeopardize the work we were doing at Influencers Church.

There were three major political parties at the time. Each had a particular agenda. Our addition would make four. Most people currently part of the political landscape dismissed our claims and figured we were just talk. . That's okay. I've been underestimated many, many times.

My Dad became the face of the movement and party. My job was to be the strategist and fundraiser. Typically, this is a team of people backed by big dollars and large staffs. We had neither, but that didn't stop us. We ran the campaign mostly out of our own house with very little money and no prior experience, and yet we knew what God had called us to do, so we moved forward trusting in His providence and divine provision.

I think it's interesting how quick we sometimes dismiss God's supernatural work in us because we can't see how all the details are going to come together. How are we going to find the money? Who is going to manage all the details? Will we know what to do in the heat of the moment?

All of these questions stem from fear and intimidation, whether it is fear of people or institutions. The Enemy is counting on us to count ourselves out because the task seems impossible. Yet, the very reason it is God's call is because it is impossible.

God had just freed His children from captivity in Egypt. They came to this land looking for food and ended up becoming slaves. Now, through a series of divinely inspired events, Pharaoh decided to set them free for fear of what might be next.

They left Egypt and found themselves trapped between a regretful Egyptian army and the Red Sea. The Israelites complained that Moses had led them away from the comforts of their homes only to be slaughtered by their oppressors. In that moment, God told Moses to raise his hands, and God made it possible for them to cross this body of water on dry land.

Later, the people became hungry. They again complained to Moses about how much better it was back in Egypt. God gave them bread and meat from heaven. They were able to eat until they were completely satisfied.

This back and forth goes on and on. If you're honest with yourself, it continues today in your life too. You ask God to do something big, and then in the midst of His movement in your life, you question whether or not it is possible. You must recognize this cycle of reasoning and keep it from limiting the authority you clearly have to accomplish whatever it is God has in mind for you.

God allowed me to move outside the boundaries of my role as a pastor and offered me the chance to influence my world. He took someone with almost no political experience (and not very deep pockets) and made it all work. What would I have missed out on if I had decided that the God of all creation couldn't accomplish the dreams He had given me? The truth is He wants to take you to new places too.

You are not limited by the time, money, or opportunity that you continue to use as an excuse for why God can't use you.

You are not limited by the time, money, or opportunity that you continue to use as an excuse for why God can't use you. You are, on the other hand, limited by your refusal to live in the authority God has already given you. Your denial results in people, places, and resources that become just out of your reach.

If you want to see God open doors and take you places others can't go, trust in the authority that is already within you. And when He takes you to new places, know that it is not only to bring glory to Himself but to remind you that He alone is the source of your victory and authority.

Day 17

AUTHORITY IS GREATER
THAN ANY FORCE THAT
MAY OPPOSE YOU

Politics is a vicious game. It will eat you alive if you're not careful. And the attacks are not always easily tied back to a particular party. It gets even more complicated when you try to introduce a new voice in the midst of already established voices, personalities, and processes.

Never underestimate the power that authority can give you, even if your power is only temporary. It can be used as a destructive weapon against an opponent, or it can be joined together against someone or something that challenges the very source of where established parties get their power. Politics is ugly and complicated, which is why most people are satisfied to sit on the sidelines and complain, rather than get in the game and take action.

If authority gave us permission to start Family First and authority gave us access to places other people can't seem to go, then we would also have to trust that this God-given authority would overcome any force that might prevent us from succeeding. I want to be sure that I make an important statement as this story unfolds. The authority we were given to start Family First did not come from our minds, strength, ingenuity, or engineering. It was a dream that God placed on the hearts of His people. Whatever you think about this story, God was at the center of every turn, making it possible for us to continue to move forward.

There were three important obstacles that we had to getting someone elected to represent this new party: money, communications strategy, and public perception. We needed money to run this campaign. It wasn't going to be cheap, but we knew that it was possible.

It wasn't the first time in my life when I've had to raise money for a particular project or cause. That is part of the life of a pastor. This opportunity was no different except that I wouldn't and couldn't use church resources to help fund it.

My role as co-founder was not connected in any way to my role as a pastor. It had to be separate both for integrity reasons and pragmatic reasons to protect the church from media manipulation and attack. This was a vision that I had to carry as an individual, not as a pastor.

Secondly, we had to have good communications strategy. We needed a team of people to help us do that. We needed memorable slogans, professionally filmed commercials, and a website where people who were curious about what we were doing could learn more and join our efforts. If this was going to work, we needed a strong effort at the grassroots level. Technology was going to be at the center of everything we were doing.

Last, we had to have a plan to manage how the media painted perceptions of us to the general public. I want to state that I'm not anti-media. I applaud journalists and believe they are often the only people connecting the dots for their readership when everyone seems to have an agenda. Unfortunately, journalists are not above or exempt from having agendas too. Sometimes journalists are mouthpieces for particular parties. This is how established parties are able to reinforce their ideas so succinctly, efficiently, and cast such a wide net over the general public.

I don't blame them, but I also knew that we had to be careful how we dealt with them. They had the power to shape the perception of a much larger audience than the one we had depended on to get us to this point. If we were going to make a successful bid for political office, we needed as many people to join our cause as possible.

Money, communications, and perception combined would either accelerate our adoption as a legitimate political force, or would plummet us into the depths of irrelevance, never to be heard from again. I promise I'm not overly dramatizing the situation. There was a lot at stake.

Not only was there a lot at stake, but also everyone—it seemed—wanted us to fail. They wanted to see us fall flat on our faces. I don't believe it was because they were mean people, though some were. I think it was because our success would force them to tighten up their positions and recognize that people weren't limited to working within established government. The idea of reform is so contagious—as we have witnessed throughout history—that no matter how powerful one person or a group of people might be at any given moment—the power of the people retains the right to change the course of events at any time.

There is no stronger force to confront than people who have banded together under the banner of conviction with the intent of initiating change. This is the fabric of revolutions, and it terrifies the ruling party.

You may not feel the push to start a political party. The opponents you face may not want to stop you from challenging a powerful, established system, but you may feel trapped. You may feel restless and want more. Only you're not sure if you can stand up to your boss and ask for a raise, confront your spouse about his or her addiction, or work through personal debt that seems to be crushing you at every turn. You feel stuck. You may be making a million dollars a year as a corporate executive, but you can still feel trapped. You may be a fast food worker with little hope for earning more than minimum wage.

When you claim the authority you have in Christ, you can do things you never thought were possible.

The Enemy wants you to believe that the force holding you back is greater than what it really is. When you claim the authority you have in Christ, you can do things you never thought were possible. I'm a pastor, and I started a political party. How absurd is that? What does God want to do through you? More importantly, what is standing in your way from claiming your rightful place and position of authority today?

Nothing will remain standing in the way when you are acting in obedience and following God, even in the face of impossible opposition. As the Psalmist proclaims, "Even though I walk through valley of the shadow of death, I will fear no evil, for you are with me" (Ps. 23:4). If death can't separate you from God, then neither can the circumstances of your life or the substance of the opposition that stands against you.

Claim your authority and watch God part the opposition just like He did the water for the children of Israel on their way to the Promised Land.

Day 18

⦙·—·⦙

AUTHORITY GIVES YOU CLARITY, DISCERNMENT, AND CONFIDENCE

G oing to the bank for most people is a normal routine. With the invention of the ATM and drive-through banking, rarely does anyone have to go into a bank for routine transactions but sometimes it's necessary. On one such particular day, I was with my oldest son, Mark, who was barely two years old at the time. I have three sons, and they are all different. Mark is by far the most energetic and active of the three.

At two. he never sat still, was always curious, and constantly wanted to explore his world. Most of the time his energy made him a lot of fun to be with. Sometimes it made him challenging to manage.

While standing in line this day, I suddenly realized that we were in the midst of danger. I heard the door of the bank burst open as armed gunmen with stockings over their faces started screaming and shouting for everyone to get on the ground. It was like something you might see on a movie or action-packed TV show. The bank was being robbed!

As I obeyed their orders and lay on the ground the next thought that ran through my mind was to make sure Mark was safe. Mark had been playing at the children's table and was stranded halfway between where I was lying and the gunman who stood menacingly only a few feet behind him. I needed him to be as still as possible so we wouldn't draw any attention to ourselves. I was in full-on parent protection mode. Taking a bullet for my family wouldn't have given me any reason to pause, but I wanted to avoid that scenario at all costs.

My eyes connected with Mark who was as still as I had ever seen him. I motioned to him to continue to look right at me and to not take his eyes off of me. It was the only thing I knew to do while we all laid on the floor hoping to survive this horrific experience.

Fear had overtaken me. All I could think about what how were we going to make it out of this alive. The gunmen paced around the bank, shouting orders, and growing more nervous and less patient as time progressed.

The first thing that came out of my mouth was the name Jesus. There is so much power in that name and on that occasion, I experienced something I have never experienced before or since. I felt the power of God come all over me and suddenly all fear—all intimidation—just vanished and in its place was complete peace and confidence.

I started a conversation with the robber by asking him if I could get my son. Now you have to understand that the place was in complete chaos. The robber answered me and told me that Mark would be ok. Then I started having conversations in my mind about whether I should get up and rebuke this guy in Jesus' name.

My mind flashed forward to the next day's newspaper headline. I could see it clearly: "Pastor Successfully Talks Down Gunman." The only thing that stopped me that day from confronting the man with the gun was my son's safety. I wasn't completely sure if this was God's way of getting on the front page, or the devil's tactic to have me killed.

Thankfully, we all made it out of that terrible situation alive.

Sometimes I think back on the situation and think about how absolutely crazy it was for me to address the man directly. I still don't fully understand what made me think I could do that.

It is clear that fear offered temporary power to the gunman, which gave him the ability to direct others to follow his wishes and fulfill his demands. The keyword, though, is temporary. Once the bubble of fear was burst, he no longer had any authority. His only recourse was to escape.

That's how fear works. It presumes upon us in a way that seems credible and certain when it is really an illusion. Fear depends on confusion, doubt, and second-guessing to keep you from living a life of victory and power.

> It really doesn't matter who or what is holding you back. Whatever it is, it's not as powerful as it wants you to think it is.

When you exercise authority and dominion, you reject the confusion, doubt, and second-guessing fear injects into the situation. It is in that moment when you then begin to see things as they are, which is often different than your first impression. This is what liberation from fear can bring into your life.

You may never have experienced a bank robbery before or confronted a dangerous gunman, but there is someone or something in your life that is holding you hostage. I don't know what it is. Truthfully, you may be the only one—besides God—who knows what is keeping you from the abundant life Jesus promised those who choose to follow Him.

It really doesn't matter who or what is holding you back. Whatever it is, it's not as powerful as it wants you to think it is. You may be convinced that confronting this fear or this person may cause you to put your life in danger. Let me suggest that a life held hostage to people and circumstances is no life at all.

Authority gives you clarity, discernment, and confidence. These three things are necessary to claim the full, abundant life we crave in our souls. Clarity allows you to see things as they are; discernment helps you know what your next step will be; and confidence gives you the courage to act.

You likely know and can name the fear that is holding you hostage. You probably know exactly what you need to do. Authority will allow you to act in confidence, knowing the power of God rests within you. Freedom is yours, and no one can take that from you.

Captivity is not God's plan for your life. There is a way out. Nothing can keep you out of the reach of God's presence, nor prevent you from experiencing God's power in your life right now. What you think may cost you your life and security is the very thing that will give you life and security. It was true for me in the bank that day, and it is true for you today.

Stand up, speak out, and believe.

Day 19

AUTHORITY ALLOWS YOU TO EXERCISE INFLUENCE

The Bible talks about a deal the children of Israel tried to make with Nahash, the king of the Ammonites. This was right after Saul was made king. Twitter didn't exist in the ancient world, so it took time for word to spread. Also, Israel was an emerging nation. While the majority wanted a king, not everyone was ready to give up their freedom to serve someone they barely knew—if at all.

There are a few things you need to understand about the ancient world. One, there were no peace treaties. You conquered or were conquered. This is one reason why the Old Testament seems to be filled with violence. Two, when you were conquered, you either became slaves or were annihilated. Neither was something to be celebrated. Third, there was no third party to appeal to and no rules of engagement to follow.

King Nahash was going to declare war on the city of Jabesh Gilead.

The people were afraid and assumed he would win. We're not told why they might have felt like that, but I would guess that they sized up the Ammonites and recognized that a victory might be just as bloody as a defeat. Instead of remembering that they were the chosen people of God, they looked around and decided that an attempt to compromise might be the best approach. This often happens to us after being intimidated and facing fear for a long time. The Bible tells us that Nahash the Ammonite had besieged the city. To besiege something means to keep up the pressure for a long time. It's the slow crush of a python squeezing the life out of its victim. Fear and intimidation besiege us. They attempt to crush and squeeze the life of God out of us, until we stop thinking clearly about who we are and start contemplating all kinds of compromise. We start to downsize our dreams and cut corners. We start to think about quitting our job or even contemplate divorce.

King Nahash offered a compromise, but it wasn't pretty. He was willing to leave them alone if they allowed him to gouge out everyone's right eye. The leaders of Israel asked for seven days to consider the terms of the compromise. I'm not sure what they were going to do for seven days. It certainly wouldn't have taken me seven days to figure out what my response was going to be.

Saul—the recently selected king—received word about the compromise, stepped in, plotted against the Ammonites, and ultimately defeated them. In the meantime, Saul secured his place of authority and influence as the first king of Israel. The rest—as they say—is history.

I want to circle back around to the proposal that King Nahash offered as terms of the compromise. It is beyond me why some were willing to consider his proposal that I'm sure he offered without any thought that they might accept the terms.

He wanted them to give up one eye, one part of their vision. Not their entire vision. Just some of it. And they were willing to entertain the idea of living the rest of their lives with only half of their vision because, sadly, fear had made them think that this was their best option!

As outlandish as this compromise might seem to you, the reality is

The good news is that even if you have allowed fear to cause you to give up influence, dominion, and authority in your life, you can reclaim it.

when you allow fear to rule your life, you have already accepted a similar compromise. Rather than living in the victory that is clearly yours, you settle for only half of your inheritance as a child of God.

When you compromise, you lose more than half of your vision. You lose your ability to see clearly. Think about what it might be like to lose one eye. Someone without one eye has difficulty judging depth, distance, and speed. Your ability to process what is taking place and react is impaired. You will never be the same. Some of the most unhappy people in this world have compromised so much in their lives that they can't remember when they first decided that compromise was an acceptable option.

The good news is that even if you have allowed fear to cause you to give up influence, dominion, and authority in your life, you can reclaim it. The thread of redemption is a present reality, not just in the midst of our eternal salvation. It daily helps us overcome fear and intimidation. Redemption gives us the confidence we need to believe God can and does work through us to accomplish abundantly more than we ever thought possible.

You may have given into your fear yesterday, but you don't have to give in again today. You may have given up half your vision yesterday, but God can restore your sight to its original condition today. You may have given up half of your dreams, but you can influence the outcome of your life today. You may have given up half of your influence, but you can discover that what was lost has now been found.

No one aspires to *almost* make a difference. No one wants to *almost* win a race. No one plans to *almost* get hired for the perfect job. No one makes it to the end of their life celebrating what they didn't fully achieve.

It's time for you to take aim. It's time for you to stop feeling pressured to wait, wonder, and worry about tomorrow. It's time for you to direct your energy toward one singular effort and refuse to be intimidated anymore.

I want you to take this book and stand in front of a mirror. What do you see? Do you see someone who has the power to influence, or do you see someone who has been influenced to stay behind and check out? Do you see someone who has been marked with the signature of the king, or do you see someone who has been marked as damaged goods? Do you see someone God believes in and has big plans for, or do you see someone who has sold out half of his or her influence in an effort to compromise and accept less than what God intended?

It's time for you to rise up. Stop allowing yourself to compromise. Losing half of what God has given you is not acceptable terms to live by, and it is not the only option available to you. You have been given permission to fly. So spread your wings and take flight. See the world through the eyes of God, and you, too, will discover that the power and authority to influence begins where your fear ends.

Day 20

•──••

AUTHORITY GIVES YOU
THE ABILITY TO POSSESS
WHAT IS RIGHTFULLY YOURS

I t's been almost a decade since I was elected to be on the national executive board of our church movement in Australia, which provides oversight to more than 1,100 churches including Hillsong church, Influencers Church, and Planetshakers, just to name a few of the more well known ones. Brian Houston was the president of the ACC when I was elected in 2001. I remember the night as if it were yesterday. Larry Stockstil was preaching the last night of the conference. I was thrilled to have the opportunity to hear him preach, but I never expected to feel a prompt to respond during the altar call.

Larry is a powerful, compelling preacher. I had heard him before, but that night his message hit me right between the eyes. There are times— and it may sound strange coming from a pastor and preacher—when a message feels like it is directed right at me. Have you ever felt that way?

As a rule, I pay very close attention to what is being said when I start to feel that way. It usually is the Holy Spirit trying to get my attention because He wants to say something important to me. Intuition is a part of the human dimension that God uses to point our attention back to Him.

I remember closing my eyes and seeing two hands inside me stretching me. This was not someone trying to take my life. Rather, these hands were stretching my capacity for more authority. It was supernatural and surreal all at the same time. I walked away that night feeling as though I had encountered God, not realizing that something was going to take place in the next few weeks that would challenge my newly gained authority.

The week following that event, I came under the most incredible intimidation of my entire life. It lasted for almost ten weeks and for the first four weeks, I felt helpless. Yes, the guy writing this book still struggles with fear at times and even hesitates to accept the authority God has given me in my own life. That's not weakness; I'm just human. .

About five weeks after the national confer-ence, I started to realize I was allowing fear to stop me in my tracks. Rather than our goal being to eliminate fear completely, the goal should be to develop a plan of action and a level of confidence that refuses to allow fear to grip your life and limit your influence and authority. This is why under-standing the role of authority in our lives is such a critical step in the breakthrough process.

> *Authority is an important concept and a fundamental reality you must come to grips with if you are going to understand the process of overcoming whatever power is trying to hold you back from the life God wants for you.*

The moment I realized I had the power to change my posture, I resolved to do just that. I wasn't going to sit on the sidelines and wallow in my fear knowing so many others felt helpless and needed to be encouraged and empowered.

I resolved not to surrender my vision or authority, so I went on a forty-day Daniel fast. (We'll talk more about the discipline of fasting and its role in breakthrough living later in this book.) In fact, I preached a series to our church on this very subject. There was no way I was backing away from fear. While I was enduring intimidation and pushing toward breakthrough, I was determined to help others continue to be liberated from their fear and intimidation too.

Something happened in the midst of that forty-day fast in regards to my battle with intimidation that is hard to explain to anyone, let alone put on paper. I saw God move in some of the most incredible ways following that experience. I believe God wants that for you too. You see, I began to understand that I didn't have to work up the feeling of authority, I didn't have to fake or pretend I had authority, I didn't have to try to earn that authority, I simply had to get the revelation that my relationship with Jesus gave me that authority. I already had it, it was rightfully mine!

You've been *given* authority and that authority is greater than any power that is against you. No matter how big it seems today, you have authority to deal with it. Jesus says, "I have given you authority to overcome all the power of the enemy" (Luke 10:18). The word power is the Greek word *dunamis*. It is where we get our word dynamite. When Jesus made this statement in Luke 10, He was telling us that authority is greater than any power the Enemy might use against us this side of heaven.

Authority is an important concept and a fundamental reality you must come to grips with if you are going to understand the process of overcoming whatever power is trying to hold you back from the life God wants for you. You can't give up. The road will be hard. It may be dark at times. There will be uncertainty. There will be doubt.

God does not give you things that will vanish or that are temporary. God gives you things that will last forever.

But I write these words today as an encouragement to you that I have seen the other side, I have experienced breakthrough, and I have been set free. The good news is that many fears have completely left me, and most of the intimidation I used to feel is gone. But it didn't just disappear; it was a process of resolve, faith, boldness, and strategy that started with the understanding that the authority I needed was already rightfully mine—it had been transferred to me through my relationship with Jesus.

Liberation is available to you today. You can have a life that is abundant and free. Whatever you are afraid of, whoever you think is holding you back, you need to tell them that you have been given authority in Christ to claim the life that is rightfully yours.

That life doesn't guarantee that you'll be rich and powerful as defined by the world. Those things are only temporary. We were all reminded of that in 2008 with the global economic meltdown. Who you are in the pecking order of a corporation or the size of your net worth on paper can vanish in an instant.

God does not give you things that will vanish or that are temporary. God gives you things that will last forever. He has given you all the power and position you need to overcome whatever fear and intimidation is holding you back. Authority is the key, and it is yours today.

In the coming days, we'll be unpacking more about God, His nature, and what He has planned for your life. I believe the roles that fear and authority play in your life will become even more evident to you as you grow in your understanding about God's desire to bless you and use you for things you never thought possible. It's going to be a powerful ten days of discovery as we explore the truth about God in relation to overcoming fear and intimidation. Are you ready?

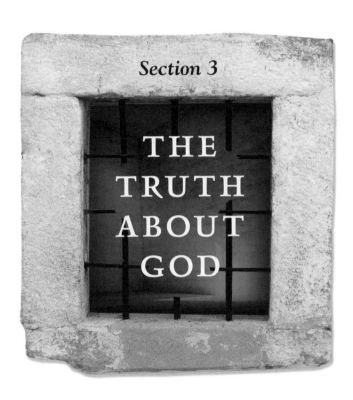

Section 3

THE
TRUTH
ABOUT
GOD

Day 21

GOD HAS A BLUEPRINT FOR YOUR LIFE

(THE ENEMY HAS ONE TOO)

David is one of my favorite characters in the Bible. I can particularly relate to the raw emotions and thoughts he penned in Psalms and with his story of dogged determination to please God but coupled with his human failings and weakness. David was a man chosen by God, who wasn't perfect but who won the battle to overcome his weaknesses and live out his life with purpose and meaning. God chose David to be king because he was a man after His own heart, and he was chosen to replace someone who missed God's plan and purpose for his life, Saul. David, because of his close relationship with God, was a man who understood that God had a plan for his life, and that plan involved following closely after God and staying connected to him. He didn't always achieve this, but he always came back to it. He provides a great example for those who may be struggling to stay the course.

The background to David's appointment to king begins with Saul. Saul was Israel's first king. Before Israel was a nation, it was a confederation of twelve different tribes named after the sons of Jacob. The people of Israel wanted a king very badly because they wanted to be more like the other nations they encountered. God eventually gave in to their repeated requests.

Samuel was the prophet of God given the task of anointing Saul as the first king. What an honor that must have been! Can you imagine what it must have been like to be given the responsibility of choosing Israel's first king? Samuel must have been excited and overwhelmed all at the same time.

Prophets were very important in the ancient world because it was through them that God spoke to His people. God's children didn't have easy access to God's Word like we do today with our Bibles. They also didn't have preachers who proclaimed truth on a weekly basis. They did have religious and temple leaders, but their job was largely designed to maintain traditions and interpret the Law of Moses.

The ancient world was a kill-or-be-killed environment. It wasn't safe to be an independent people group, apart from a larger nation-state that could share resources to equip for battle, support commerce, and keep the peace. This is why having a king was so important for the people of Israel. They wanted the other people groups they encountered to know that they were not independent but part of a much larger entity.

When Saul disobeyed God, Samuel declared that God would no longer allow him to be king. That seems harsh, doesn't it? One way to look at the story is to say that God didn't get His way and Saul didn't do exactly as God instructed, so God punished him. Another way to understand it is to see that God wanted Saul to be king. It was when he tried to do things on his own that he failed.

David would become king because Saul chose not to follow God's plan for his life. I don't want you to miss this learning opportunity. Saul's decision to not follow God's plan for his life, cost him influence, authority, and power. When we give in to fear and intimidation, we sidestep or limit God's plan for our lives.

Did you know that God carefully designed you, and He has a special plan for your life? You were created to accomplish something very special. David wrote about this in Psalm 139:13–16.

> For you created my inmost being;
> you knit me together in my mother's womb.
> I praise you because I am fearfully
> and wonderfully made;
> your works are wonderful,
> I know that full well.
> My frame was not hidden from you
> when I was made in the secret place.
> When I was woven together in the depths of the earth,
> your eyes saw my unformed body.
> All the days ordained for me
> were written in your book
> before one of them came to be.

What an important confession on the part of David. Saul's decision to disobey God because of the pressure he was facing cost him his authority and dominion. Because of his unwillingness to follow God's plan, it cost him everything! I believe David understood that God's plan was to place Saul as king for his entire life.

God has a plan for our lives, a plan He has every intention of making reality. We do have the power to ignore God's plan. This forces God's hand in a way. I'm not suggesting that God is limited by our human power. To believe that would be to limit God. What I am saying is that God wants to use us but we must also be willing to follow along. When we choose not to, we disrupt God's plan and miss out on His blessing.

God has a plan for our lives, a plan He has every intention of making reality.

Make no mistake about it. The Enemy has a plan for your life too. He had one for Saul. The Enemy wanted to limit Saul's authority and dominion. Unfortunately, the Enemy's plan to cause Saul to compromise on his obedience to God's plan was successful. The cost was substantial, and Saul's life was cut short on the battle field when, after being wounded, he fell on his own sword rather than allow his enemies to kill him. What a sad ending to such a promising beginning!

God has a plan that He carefully crafted for you. He gave you skills, talents, and abilities to do great things. His plan may not include making you king of a particular nation, but that doesn't mean God doesn't have big plans for you in mind. When we choose not to believe that we have value, meaning, and purpose, we reject God's design and forfeit His blessing.

Worse, when we choose anything other than God's plan for our lives, the Enemy succeeds. He knows that his efforts are limited. One day Jesus will come back, and his ability to interrupt God's plan will end for eternity. In the meantime, he is hard at work trying to limit our lives.

I wonder if your life is like that of Saul. Have you rejected God's plan and forfeited His blessing? The good news is that if you have, that doesn't mean you have to continue to do so. God's plan is one of hope and redemption. God's plan doesn't end with our disobedience but is filled with the opportunity to be restored. That's what God wants for you. God still loves you and has big plans for you.

Day 22

GOD CREATED YOU TO
MULTIPLY, NOT MAINTAIN

Saul's rejection of God's plan for his life led to regret, suffering, and pain. An unlikely person succeeded him. While God had blessing and authority in mind, Saul's choices prevented him from experiencing the abundant favor God wanted to show him. It is an unfortunate commentary for the first king of Israel.

The good news is that God will not be deterred from accomplishing His will, even if we choose not to participate in the way He originally designed. The focal point of the story now shifts from Saul to David. Samuel comes to the house of Jesse, David's father, under clear instruction from God that one of Jesse's sons would be the next king.

Jesse, as the story unfolds, carefully prepares his sons for Samuel's arrival. I can only imagine what it must have been like to receive word that God's prophet was coming to your house to choose the next king. The preparations must have been extremely elaborate.

We do know that Jesse had eight sons. Upon Samuel's arrival, seven of the eight were paraded in front of Samuel so that he could choose one of them to be king. I suspect that Jesse had each son shower, put on special clothes, and maybe even perform a particular talent. Perhaps they each shared a story of their heroism in hopes of capturing the imagination of Samuel so that they could secure the throne of Israel.

Only, Samuel wasn't impressed by any of the sons that Jesse put before him. In fact, Scripture says that Samuel turned to Jesse and said, "The Lord has not chosen these . . . Are these all the sons you have?" (1 Sam 16:10–11). You probably could have heard a pin drop in the room. How could Samuel reject all seven of Jesse's sons? Even worse, Samuel's question suggests that Jesse did not represent every son before God's prophet to be considered and perhaps chosen.

I wonder why Jesse didn't call for David. Maybe Jesse wanted to protect his youngest son from his first experience of rejection. Maybe he just wanted to spare his son the drama knowing that one of his older brothers would ultimately be chosen to be king. Whatever the reason, it never occurred to Jesse that David could be God's choice.

God's plan often includes choosing the most unlikely candidate and placing that person in a position of authority and dominion. He does this for the purpose of bringing about His glory on earth. Paul writes to the church at Corinth and says, "But God chose the foolish things of the world to shame the wise; God chose the weak things of the world to shame the strong" (1 Cor. 1:27).

> God's plan often includes choosing the most unlikely candidate and placing that person in a position of authority and dominion.

Wherever you are today, whatever the circumstances, however you arrived at where you are today, you need to know that God wants more for you. He doesn't want to leave you behind, nor has he already done so. God has not forgotten about you. On the contrary, God has His eye on you and has big plans for you.

You may not be the strongest, smartest, or even the most likely choice. Just because you weren't the star athlete in high school, voted most likely to succeed, or ever considered popular doesn't mean God hasn't reached down from heaven and placed His hand of blessing on your life. Fear and intimidation, uncertainly and doubt, circumstances and situations may bring roadblocks, but nothing can prevent you from being chosen, blessed, and uplifted by God's favor.

So if Jesse didn't bring all of his sons before Samuel to be considered to succeed Saul as king, where was David? David had obeyed his father's wishes and was in the field tending to the sheep. He left the house that day knowing he was an unlikely candidate for God's divine favor and would probably spend the rest of his life in the fields tending to sheep. Being a shepherd is not a bad way to live, but it certainly was different from being the king of Israel.

It was David's willingness to be obedient to his father's wishes that proved he had been set apart for something big. What David was willing to do was the very reason Saul had walked away from God's favor. Obedience is the qualifying characteristic of those who experience the abundant life.

God chose David. The fact that Jesse made the decision to not include him in the lineup didn't prevent God from showing him favor. Even if you don't feel like you have been given a fair shake in life, it doesn't mean you are outside of God's ability to bless you in an unbelievable way. God wants to multiply what you have. It may not come at the time you want it to come or in the way you want it to play out, but it will come when you are obedient.

God is not limited by this world. He created it. While we are bound by the limited nature of life, God is infinite in power, authority, dominion, and blessing. He wants to do things in and through you that you have yet to even consider possible. The lie that fear tells us is that what we see is what we get. Not true. It wasn't true of Samuel. It wasn't true for Saul. It wasn't true for David. It's not true for you, either.

God doesn't want to keep you in the fields tending sheep. He wants to multiply your life and use you to accomplish more than you ever thought possible. Fear may give you reason to pause, but the authority of God Almighty will give you the patience to endure and the strength to overcome.

Day 23

GOD IS NOT LIMITED BY YOUR CIRCUMSTANCES

David was not present when God's prophet came to his house. He was sent away by Jesse, his father, because Jesse didn't think that David had any chance of being the chosen one. As far as his father was concerned, Samuel had seven other better choices to choose from.

Samuel knew God had led him to the right place, which is why he asked Jesse if he had any more sons. In spite of not being present, Samuel knew someone was missing. In spite of his father sending him away, David still was in the running. In spite of David being the most unlikely candidate, God chose him.

I love how Samuel reacts when he discovers that David, while not present, is not far away. He won't let the celebration meal start until David returns. Keep in mind that Jesse was not sticking his head out the back door and yelling for David to come in the house. One of Jesse's servants—most likely—is asked to go find David. It is likely that no one knew exactly where David was. They knew the general territory he might be in, but the servants would have to search for him.

While they searched for David, Samuel asked them to wait. I bet the atmosphere in the room was so thick you could cut it with a knife. All of David's brothers were looking at their father, and their father was looking back at them. No words, just a questioning and anticipation at what might happen next.

Jesse probably began to wonder if God would punish him for keeping David away if he was, in fact, the next king of Israel. How would he ever explain this to David? Would David hold a grudge against him? If Jesse pleaded for forgiveness, would David give it to him? And how was he going to explain this to his brothers?

The time it took to find David, explain to him what was going on, and for David to return must have seemed like an eternity. In the meantime, Samuel, Jesse, seven of his sons, and whoever else was in the house, stood and waited for what might be the coming of the next king. This was not the first time the people of God waited in anticipation of a king, nor would it be the last time.

Upon David's arrival, God confirmed for Samuel that he was the one he had been sent to find. The Bible says God told Samuel, "Rise and anoint him; he is the one" (1 Sam. 16:12). David went from being sent away to take care of the family chores for the day to being anointed Israel's next king.

There is nothing that can prevent you from being used by God in a way that will change the world forever.

Being anointed with oil was an important symbol that ancient societies used to signify someone had been set-aside for something very special. This act performed by God's prophet was equivalent to God speaking in that moment and declaring David as His chosen one. There was no doubt about whom David was from that point on. He was God's replacement for Saul.

Have you ever considered yourself anointed by God? Has it ever occurred to you that God has chosen you for something special? A prophet of God may not have come to your house and poured oil over your head, but God has chosen you. You may not have competed with your siblings to be king, but God has chosen you. You may never have even felt special, but God has chosen you.

Because God has chosen you, He will lift you up so that you can do exceedingly more than you ever thought possible. If God has anointed you, then nothing can stand in your way. There is nothing that can prevent you from being used by God in a way that will change the world forever.

I believe there are three things most people perceive as holding them back from the life they dream about: expectations of others, experience, and circumstances. It is tough to endure the expectations of others, especially when it doesn't match your passions, dreams, and desires. God did not give you those things so that you could experience regret; He gave you those things so you would not be held back by the expectations of others.

Experience also seems to be a common reason people give for why their life hasn't turned out the way they wanted. Maybe you believe you don't have the right education, the right job title, or the right amount of money or opportunity to achieve what God has given you a desire to accomplish. It is ironic that experience never seemed to matter in Scripture when God chose someone to do something special.

Our circumstances remind us of the choices we have made and perhaps the choices that have been made for us. In the quiet moments, we hope for something better. We want to move to another neighborhood. We want to ask for the promotion at work. We want to change the direction our life has been heading. The reason we don't ask God for those things is that we don't believe the Creator of the Universe has power over what we can see, taste, touch, and feel today.

Your circumstances, experience, and the expectations of others are not enough to hold you back. You have been anointed by God. You are royalty. You have all the resource you need, all the strength you desire, and all the wisdom that you've ever wished for at your disposal.

God is not limited by your circumstances. Don't let the Enemy fool you into believing that you are limited. Break free! Allow the Spirit of the Lord to come upon you just as it did to David at the moment of his anointing. The only thing that is holding you back is your willingness to say yes to God.

Day 24

GOD IS A GOD
OF SECOND CHANCES

Samuel went looking for a king and found a shepherd boy. He was commanded by God to find Saul's successor and discovered him in the fields doing chores. He went unsure of what he would find but was confident in what God revealed.

God tells Samuel in the process of his examination of the seven eldest sons of Jesse, "Do not consider his appearance . . . The Lord does not look at the things man looks at. Man looks at the outward appearance, but the Lord looks at the heart" (1 Sam. 16:7). How many times are we preoccupied with the outward things when we should revel in the idea that we are already the objects of God's affection? We have already been chosen.

This is one of the most significant moments in David's journey to be king. If we're not familiar with David's story, we might think that David's life after this point is, as they say, all downhill from here. It would be nice to think that he was welcomed into the royal court by Saul who quickly and ceremoniously handed over all authority to David. Then, of course, we want to believe that David went on to live a full life that was without poor decisions and failure. It might be easy to wrap a bow around a story like that, but David's life unfolded very differently than what I have just described.

The first thing that comes to mind when people are told that God has chosen them to do amazing things is that some decision they made in the past will keep them from experiencing the future God wants to give them. Nothing could be further from the truth. The God of the Bible is a God of second chances.

God is not a "one and done" wizard waiting to zap you every time you make a mistake. He is not waiting and watching to catch you doing something wrong. Rather, God is a loving God who created you because He wanted to have a relationship with you.

Your life isn't perfect, nor is mine. You haven't always made good choices, nor have I. You may have lacked commitment to your faith and the people you love, and so have I. The Enemy wants to convince you that you've been disqualified from God's plan. He wants you to throw in the towel and hang it up.

Why do you think the Enemy wants you to consider yourself useless? Because if he can convince you to sit on the sidelines, he doesn't have to worry about how God will empower you to do supernatural things. He doesn't want you to know that because it reminds him that he has already lost.

God has chosen you and has a plan for your life. He wants to take the used up, pressed down, and wrinkled parts of your life and use them as a canvas for His masterpiece.

When God says you are chosen, He already knows you are not perfect. It's not a secret to Him or to you. That's okay. He still—in spite of your past—hasn't given up on you. He still wants to use you to accomplish His will in this world.

Through a series of bad decisions, King David, the anointed one, would later commit adultery. Yes, he had sex with another man's wife. Not something you would think God's anointed would do, would you?

To complicate matters, David has her husband killed during battle, so he could marry her. Even though God didn't like or agree with David's choices, God allows him to continue to be king and continues to bless him. There were certainly consequences to David's decision, but he wasn't counted out of God's plan. In fact, you can't talk about the history of Israel without talking about David—his victories and his defeats.

The Bible reveals later that Jesus—the Messiah—comes from the line of David. Think about that. God uses David's family tree to find a place to inject Jesus as a human being into this world. If God can do that with a murderer and adulterer, what more can He do through you?

I have failed. I have come up short of God's expectations. There have been times I've doubted. I questioned whether or not I heard God correctly. Yet, God still chooses to use me to bring about His will.

I have failed Jane. I have failed my children. I have failed my church. I have failed my staff. At some point, I have disappointed, frustrated, or discouraged everyone in my life. But God hasn't counted me out.

God has chosen you and has a plan for your life. He wants to take the used up, pressed down, and wrinkled parts of your life and use them as a canvas for His masterpiece. God believes in you, and so do I.

You may have made some bad choices, but you're not out of the game. You may have been divorced, fired, convicted of a crime, or told you were worth absolutely nothing. I tell you today that God has given you life, not so you can wallow in your defeat, but so you can stand up, knock the mud off your shoes, and move forward. God has more in store for you. He is not finished with you.

God anointed David, an unlikely king. God blessed David, an adulterer and murderer. God used David, an unforgettable player in God's plan.

The Enemy wants you to believe that your past determines your future. He wants you to become so consumed with guilt and shame that you take yourself out of the game. This is what fear and intimidation are designed to accomplish.

God, on the other hand, is ready to give you a second chance. He wants to bless others by blessing you. If God didn't count David out, He hasn't counted you out either.

Day 25

❧

GOD'S PRESENCE
BRINGS AN AWARENESS
OF YOUR DEEPEST FEARS

Just because Samuel had anointed David as king didn't mean that Saul was immediately removed from his throne. In fact, Saul stays in the picture until his tragic death. Saul's life reads more like a Greek tragedy than what we might expect from the Bible. His life proves that daytime TV has nothing on the drama in the Bible.

Perhaps the most well-known part of David's life is his encounter and victory over Goliath, the overgrown giant who fought for the Philistines, who were enemies of the children of Israel. I think there are some elements within this event that offer some important insight into how God can use you in the midst of your fear and intimidation. They don't have to paralyze you. In fact, He can use them to propel you toward—rather than prohibit you from—victory.

As common with most stories, two opposing forces have met for a battle. This was not unusual in the ancient world. For some of you reading this book, you feel like your life is a battleground. It seems that no matter what you do, you seem to continue to meet—and be defeated—by whatever opposes you. But I have good news for you. Keep reading!

Goliath was a big guy. The Bible says he was more than nine feet tall. (If Goliath lived today, he would be the most sought after athlete in the world.) He was the most intimidating force that the Philistines could find. I can only imagine how many times they had used his sheer size to intimidate their opponents from engaging with them in war. Not a bad strategy if your goal is to win while minimizing the loss of your people and resources. I can't blame them for their decision. Had I been a Philistine, I would have approved of using Goliath to my advantage too.

God takes us to the edge because that is the only way we'll ever understand that our lives are in His hands.

Their success rate was high enough that their arrogance created an expectation of victory. Defeat never crossed their mind. While the rest of the Philistine army stayed safely behind the front lines where Goliath trolled, Goliath began taunting the Israelites led by Saul.

To be fair, Saul was a good leader. He may have walked away from God's favor, but the children of Israel were fighters. Only Saul had never encountered an opponent like Goliath before. He wasn't sure what to do.

Goliath challenged one of the Israelites to fight him. If the Israelite won, then the Philistines would surrender. But if Goliath won, then the Israelites would surrender. After having seen so many supernatural things take place, the children of Israel stood in complete fear. The Bible says, "On hearing the Philistine's words, Saul and all the Israelites were dismayed and terrified" (1 Sam. 17:11).

I wonder what you are facing today that has you paralyzed with fear. Not only do we become aware of our fears when we face them head on, God's presence also brings us in touch with our deepest fears. God takes us to the edge because that is the only way we'll ever understand that our lives are in His hands.

As a child, you might remember singing the words, "He's got the whole world in his hands." This makes sense to us as a child, particularly if we had parents who loved us and cared for us. We form our thoughts about God at an early age. This is why it is so important for parents to set a godly example for their children.

But what about the children who didn't come from homes where they were consistently loved and cared for? From an early age, some children adapt and cope with having to be on their own and look after themselves or maybe even younger siblings. Some children grow up too fast. It's a sad commentary on modern culture and is one of the primary reasons Family First was an important political movement to begin.

I don't know what your deepest fear is, but you do. You may never have said it out loud, confessed it to your pastor or priest, or even confided such information to your spouse. It is not uncommon to meet with people who have yet to admit their fear and recognize what is intimidating them. If only they would slow down enough to put a name to what is driving them to a life of anxiety or depression.

When we do have the opportunity to face our fears, we are often left paralyzed. We're not sure what to do next, so we stand there while our fears taunt us and dare us to challenge them. Maybe God has spoken to you in a dream or through your prayer time. Maybe God is using your pastor to reveal your fear to you. Maybe God is using your closest relationships to show you what's holding you back.

This is not a critique on who you should be. God is not trying to point out where you fall short. On the contrary, God wants you to see what is holding you back, so you are ready to begin the process of breaking through. In the final section of this book, we will unpack practical steps to breakthrough. If, however, you do not recognize your biggest fear and admit what intimidates you, then you will not be ready.

The children of Israel had God—the Creator of all things and the source of every previous victory—on their side going into battle with the Philistines. Yet Goliath stopped them in their traps. One guy (Goliath) caused them to lose their senses, question their confidence, and rethink their victory plan.

This is exactly what fear does in our lives. God wants to reveal your biggest fears to you, so you can be ready to overcome. The Enemy wants to confront you with your biggest fears, so he can keep you from overcoming. Stop letting the Enemy win when you already have God on your side.

Day 26

⁘

GOD WANTS MORE FOR YOU THAN WHAT YOU HAVE AND ARE TODAY

Goliath heckles his opponents day and night for forty days. The oversized warrior that the Philistines are counting on to ensure their victory over the Israelites continues his rant without opposition. Every day he comes to the front of the battle line and challenges someone to come forward to fight him.

The Israelites, clearly frustrated but overwhelmed, never send anyone forward. To do so would certainly have ended in their demise. No one was up for a suicide mission.

David, again, is in the background. While he is tending to Saul, he is also helping his father take care of his sheep. His older brothers are part of the group assembled to fight the Philistines, which means they are also part of the group unwilling to match the daily challenge coming from Goliath.

Jesse asks David to take food to his brothers. David, being an obedient son, does exactly what his father asks him to do. He goes into the Israelite camp, finds his brothers, and delivers the food that his father sent.

While he is there dropping off the food and supplies, David hears Goliath in the background. He watches as this arrogant giant steps forward and challenges an Israelite to fight. David is confused as to why no one has stepped forward to fight this opponent.

> I'm convinced that the reason you are not living the life God has placed in your heart is because you see yourself through the eyes of other people, rather than through the eyes of God.

David asks someone standing nearby what's going on. Rumor is that Saul is offering a huge reward for someone to step forward, defeat the giant, and lead the Israelites to victory. Probably not the best military strategy, but the Israelites—and Saul—are desperate at this point.

Goliath does not intimidate David. In fact, David is a little irritated that not one of God's chosen people has stepped forward to defeat the giant. How could they have let this go on for so long? Further, David is upset that they have let an opponent—however formidable—defy the name of the Lord.

David kept expressing his disappointment that this "uncircumcised Philistine should dare defy the armies of the Lord" until someone with access to the king reports his words to Saul. Then David is called for an audience before the king.

He expresses how upset and frustrated he is at the situation, and David offers himself to step forward and challenge the giant. Saul immediately discourages David by telling him that he is too small and too young for the job.

He responds to Saul's word of caution by declaring, "You servant has killed both the lion and the bear; this uncircumcised Philistine will be like one of them, because he has defied the armies of the living God" (1 Sam. 17:36).

There is a common theme in David's life. He is consistently underestimated by others. His father sends him out to the field for chores when Samuel, God's prophet, comes to choose the next king. His brothers thank him for the food, but tell him to move back from the battle lines for safety.

Even Saul tells him he is too small and too young to fight Goliath. The strange thing is that David never hesitates; his conviction leads him to action. No amount of skepticism or discouragement from others is going to hold him back.

David never thought of himself only as a shepherd boy, a food delivery service, or a musician and subject in the king's court. He clearly remembered the anointing Samuel gave him and believed it was an authentic pronouncement by God Himself. This was the opportunity he was looking for. Not to prove himself to others, but to be obedient to what God had called him to do: lead.

God has called you to lead too. He has given you authority and dominion. When you shrink back from that, you allow God to be mocked, disregarded, and discredited. I'm convinced that the reason you are not living the life God has placed in your heart is because you see yourself through the eyes of other people, rather than through the eyes of God.

The eyes of your friends and family limit you because they are human eyes. When the Spirit comes into your life, you are given divine eyes. You are able to recognize when God is moving and the direction He is headed. Our job is to follow God's plan and obey. It's really that simple.

I wonder if you have allowed yourself to be limited for so long that the dreams God has placed in your heart have become dormant and almost forgotten. In those quiet moments, you remember but quickly dismiss your hopes and passions in the name of practicality and reason. You are so much more than you give yourself credit for.

There is a giant in your life that is taunting you on the battlefield. It's called fear. I don't know the name of that fear, but you do. You are allowing it to intimidate you and hold you back from being who God called you to be and doing what God called you to do.

Nothing in this world is beyond the reach or power of God. When Jesus ascended into heaven, He gave us His power in the person of the Holy Spirit. That Spirit lives in you. The only thing that can hold you back is the power you give the Enemy when you allow yourself to be limited by the expectations and assumptions of others.

Stop waiting for the right time. Quit making excuses. Act in the name of the God who saved you. The battle may be in play, but the war has been won. God is the victor, and He will give victory, power, and dominion to those who trust Him and believe.

God wants more for you than what you have and are today. The Enemy wants you to believe that this is as good as it gets. Don't listen to the lie anymore. If you're still not convinced that God can use you, wait until you read what happens next.

Day 27

GOD HAS GIVEN
EVERY BELIEVER A PLACE
OF INFLUENCE

David stepped forward. It probably happened before anyone knew what was about to happen. He kept getting closer and closer to the battle line and never even paused. With a sling and five smooth stones, David walked right up to Goliath.

Goliath didn't know how to react. For a moment, he had to wonder if it was a trap. Why would they send a young boy to fight? He knew it was only a matter of time before the Philistines invaded the Israelite camp and declared victory.

At first, Goliath didn't take David seriously. My guess is he probably started laughing. He may have even pointed at a few other Philistines behind him and said a few coarse remarks.

David knew what it was like to be underestimated. He didn't appreciate it coming from Goliath. It was different when it came from Saul, his father, or even his brothers. Goliath was not just challenging the Israelites; he was making fun of God. David couldn't stand it.

When David stepped forward, Goliath dismissed him. There was still time for David to scurry back to safety but there was no stopping him. He was a man on a mission. He told Goliath, "You come against me with sword and spear and javelin, but I come against you in the name of the Lord Almighty" (1 Sam. 17:45).

The Bible doesn't record Goliath's response to this declaration of war. I'd imagine that the smirk left his face and the fire in his heart burned. Goliath was done giving this boy a chance to go back to safety. If David wanted to fight, Goliath was going to give him a fight.

David continues, "This day the Lord will hand you over to me, and I'll strike you down and cut off your head . . . the whole world will know that there is a God in Israel" (1 Sam. 17:46). He was clear, concise, and spoke with conviction. No one was uncertain about David's intentions, including Goliath.

As Goliath's disposition changed, he started into his pre-battle routine. Perhaps they even circled each other as Goliath moved from side to side. I'm sure he was convinced this would be a quick and bloody ending. He was going to teach the Israelites a lesson.

David slipped into warrior mode too. In the same way that he had killed lions, bears, and whatever other animals or thieves who might threaten the life of his father's sheep, he was ready to risk his life to fight Goliath. That's what shepherds do. Without any pause or caution, a shepherd protects the life of his sheep from invasion and attack. This made the job very dangerous, so David had lived his life preparing for the unexpected.

In that moment, David went from being a lonely shepherd boy bringing his brothers some food to a peer willing to fight for his country and his God. His decision and behavior gave him a position of influence. No one could take that away from him, not even Goliath.

God has given you a position of influence too. It may not involve grabbing your sling and picking out five smooth stones to fight a giant. Nevertheless, you engage the world on a daily basis. The relationships you have, the lifestyle you live, and things you choose to invest your time, talent, and treasure in all give you influence.

Sometimes people think influence is only for political officials or military leaders. This is not true. Positions don't give you influence. Trust gives you influence. You build trust by being who you say you are and doing what you say you will do.

It's easy to recognize when someone isn't being true to themselves and who they were created to be. These people often live with a bitterness and criticism about the world that colors every part of life. In its extreme form, these people can become toxic.

Fear will always try to steer you away from becoming a person of influence. God will empower you to succeed.

When you don't exercise the influence God has given you, there is an undeniable missing piece in your life, an appetite for something else that never seems to be satisfied. You try to fill that hole with buying things, working hard, getting ahead, and taking more and more extravagant vacations. None of those things are wrong or bad, but none of those things are the path to a life of influence.

God gave David a place of influence that day because he was willing to step forward to protect the integrity of what he knew to be true. When you stand for what you know to be true, you will gain influence too. And influence is exactly God's plan for you.

Influence gives us the power to be heard. Influence gives us the ability to get in the middle of a situation and change the course of events. Influence is what allows us to speak into the lives of others. Just because you don't have a national—or international—platform with people from all over the world hanging on your every word doesn't mean you don't have a place of influence.

God has given you a unique set of talents and gifts to be used to bring Him glory. He has placed you in a unique set of circumstances with the right personal and professional experience. Why has God done that? So you can influence the outcome to expand the boundaries of the kingdom.

The Enemy wants you to believe that you don't have any influence. He knows that if you exercised your influence, then he would lose the attention of the people in your life. Worse, you might lead them to break-through so they, too, can become a person of influence.

When you refuse to accept the role God has called you to play, you give up the influence you have with the people around you. Fear will always try to steer you away from becoming a person of influence. God will empower you to succeed.

Day 28

GOD DESIGNED YOU
TO BE A FORCE OF CHANGE
IN THE WORLD

What David does next is absolutely unthinkable. While the entire Israelite and Philistine armies stand by, David and Goliath get ready to fight. The Bible says, "As the Philistine moved closer to attack him, David ran quickly toward the battle line to meet him" (1 Sam. 17:48).

David, a shepherd boy whose only reason for visiting the front lines is to obey his father and bring food to his brothers, rushes toward the Philistine's weapon of choice, Goliath. He doesn't run away from this foreboding character. Rather, he runs to him. With the increasing proximity to what causes our fear, most of us are inclined to run away, but David ran *toward* the giant! Don't give in to the temptation to run away, but stand your ground and move toward what is intimidating you.

I've seen enough fights to know that the first rule of war is to size up your opponent. If you don't think you have a chance, the second rule is to plan your escape route. There is no way that David is any physical match to Goliath. The Philistines must have thought this was going to be a quick and easy match.

But David knew that the Lord was with him. He knew that God had given him authority and influence in this situation, and he acted on every ounce of God's presence in that moment. He didn't run to the side, stop on the way, or even retreat. David rushed the giant. I wish I had had front-row seats to this match.

On the way to Goliath, David reaches into his pouch and pulls out one stone. Remember, he has five. I might have chosen to pull out a few more just in case the first one wasn't successful. David was clear and levelheaded. He reminded himself that he had done battle protecting his father's sheep. Only this time, it wasn't a wild animal or a thief wanting to kill or steal an animal; it was a giant who had called into question the very existence of David's God.

He strategically places the stone inside the sling and begins to twirl it over his head. Goliath waves his sword, pointing it directly at David's torso. In his mind, it is only going to take one swing to knock this opponent out. Unfortunately, Goliath didn't anticipate a slingshot.

It's reasonable to think that Goliath didn't give much consideration to a slingshot. He was used to fighting with the people who used swords and shields. Slingshots were for boys to use in the field. Men used real weapons. Goliath must have thought David's demise and the victory over the Israelites seemed easily within reach.

You can be a force of change in this world if you stop allowing fear to hold you back from God's plan.

When David let that stone go, all time stood still. Goliath probably never saw it coming. That rock hit Goliath right in the forehead. Moments later, Goliath falls to the ground face first. The mighty warrior is dead at the hands of a shepherd boy. The Bible says, "So David triumphed over the Philistine with a sling and a stone; without a sword in his hand he struck down the Philistine and killed him" (1 Sam. 17:50).

Seconds later the Israelites break the silence and begin cheering while the Philistines stare in disbelief. I wonder if the leader of the Philistine army ran forward to check and make sure Goliath was dead. No one—the Israelites nor the Philistines—expected Goliath to not survive this attack. David's brothers prepared themselves for the worst, and Saul probably did the same thing.

David's victory signaled the end of the Philistines' ability to hold the Israelites hostage and taunt them day and night by mocking their God. One stone accomplished more than any military assault could have hoped to accomplish. David's obedience set the children of God free from the Philistines' incessant taunting. God wants to set you free so you can free others too.

You can be a force of change in this world if you stop allowing fear to hold you back from God's plan. Right now you already possess everything you need to take the next step toward God. He wants to bless you. He wants to empower you. He wants to take you places that you've never thought possible.

You can break free from poverty. You can be promoted to that job. You can drive that car. You can be a great parent. You can be a great husband or wife.

What is standing in the way of you accepting the power and authority God wants to give you? It is money? Is it opportunity? Is it confidence? Is it experience? David was a boy who didn't blink when God called him to the frontlines to defeat Goliath. God wants to give you victory too.

Goliath wasn't just a great Philistine warrior. His character also represents the role fear and intimidation play in your life. Fear keeps you from doing what God called you to do.

Fear stands in the way of your progress and taunts you. Fear mocks God because it tries to convince you that you can't do it. Fear tells you that you're not enough. Fear tells you that it's impossible.

Paul writes, "For I am convinced that neither death nor life, neither angels nor demons, neither the present nor the future, nor any powers, neither height nor depth, nor anything else in all creation, will be able to separate us from the love of God" (Rom. 8:38–39).

How encouraging is it to know that God wants you to be a force of change in the world? He wants to use you to lift up, rescue, empower, and equip others to also be a force of change in the world. Jesus changed the world with twelve men. You, as a follower of Christ, get to be part of the legacy of that revolution today.

David's victory signaled the release of the Israelites from the fear instilled by Goliath. Jesus' victory through the resurrection releases us from the power of fear and intimidation for eternity. You no longer have to feel bound up, held back, or backed into a corner. You are a child of God, and you have been set free to create change. That change begins in your life.

We're almost ready to dig into the steps to breakthrough. Don't give up yet! Remember that those moments of intimidation are either stepping-stones or tombstones. Every time you overcome your fear, you have stepped up to another level of authority.

Day 29

GOD DESIRES TO
USE YOU TO ENLARGE
THE KINGDOM

I t must have been an unbelievable thing to watch. The headlines of the local newspaper might have read, "Young Boy Wins Battle, Defeats Goliath." Word would spread quickly. The Philistine army—in all their arrogance—must have been at a loss for words. Their entire strategy was shattered in a matter of minutes.

After killing Goliath, David walks over to the giant. There is no apparent fear in David. He knows he has won. Some might have thought that it just made Goliath pass out or faint; how could one stone from a simple slingshot kill the mighty Goliath?

Doubt was spreading through both camps. The Israelites didn't know if it was appropriate to cheer too much for fear that Goliath might not be dead. The Philistines were hoping that Goliath might show some sign of life as the seconds and minutes passed. They looked closely for a flick of the finger, but they saw nothing.

Recognizing that some were still doubting whether or not Goliath was actually dead, David walks over to him and stands next to him. Maybe he reaches over and touches him. With no response, maybe he pushes him. Both sides are leaning in, hoping for a definitive answer on whether or not Goliath is actually dead.

It occurs to David that he will have to do one more thing to ensure there is no doubt—on either side—as to whether or not this giant is dead or alive. He takes Goliath's sword, which was not a small or light one. David then cuts off Goliath's head to settle the debate and secure his victory over Goliath.

> Living a life of no more fear is not only about becoming free in this life but recognizing the seeds we can plant that have eternal implications.

I personally think that he cut off his head so that this giant who had used words to intimidate so many people could never use words again. The head symbolized the source of intimidation, words. Words are so often the prime cause of our fear and our intimidation.

Self-talk can be very destructive. People's opinions and comments can cause damage. Deal with the words and most times you'll deal with the intimidation.

When the Philistines realize their champion is dead, they know what is about to happen next. The Israelites realize God has given them the victory, so they charged the Philistines and defeated them.

David and Israel's army return home to find a celebration. News had preceded their arrival of Goliath's defeat and Israel's victory. As a sign of God's power, David brought back Goliath's head to Jerusalem and kept Goliath's armor for himself. Every time he looked at it the armor was a constant reminder to David of what God and he could achieve together. David had fought for his own life that day, but more significantly he had fought for the lives of his fellow Israelites. He had saved them from a lifetime of slavery and servitude under the Philistines. That's what God wants to do through you too! It's not only for your freedom that you are fighting for, but for the freedom of your family, your friends, and even those who you have yet to meet.

God wants to use you to enlarge the kingdom. He doesn't give you authority, dominion, and power so you can live comfortably. That's not the end game. There is nothing wrong with the pursuit of material possessions as long as it is not surpassed in your pursuit of the things of God. None of the money, power, and possessions Goliath brought to the battle would have prevented his demise.

Living a life of no more fear is not only about becoming free in this life but recognizing the seeds we can plant that have eternal implications. When we choose to live by God's plan, we will influence the people around us. They will notice our lives are not held hostage by the concerns and fears in this world.

Enlarging the kingdom is about showing others there is another way to live. Most people live consumed by fear, uncertainty, and doubt. They question their decisions, gripe about their circumstances, and complain about everything. The sad reality is that too many Christians live like that. Is it any wonder that the world looks at Christians and wonders what the Good News is that we keep talking about?

If God were a cosmic genie, then He would grant us our every wish. That's not the freedom I'm talking about. The freedom to overcome, break free, and live victoriously always results in expansion of the kingdom. If we will allow Him to work through us, then we will play a key role in how He accomplishes His plan.

David faced the fear that had brought the entire Israelite army to its knees. He didn't back down. He didn't second-guess himself. David ran toward the giant with a purpose and intention. Who do you think gave him that confidence? It was the experience of facing the lion and the bear and successfully overcoming them that gave him the preparedness and boldness to face the giant. Each time he faced the enemies that threatened him and won, his confidence in God's ability to back up his boldness with strength and success grew. He went from protecting sheep to leading an army and finally ruling over an entire nation! Each time he faced intimidation with boldness and trust, he not only had success and victory, but his confidence in God and the call on his life grew.

The lie the Enemy wants us to believe is that if we face our fear, then it will crush us. Fear and intimidation are an illusion because we already have the victory in Christ. It is ours not to be earned but exercised in the work of enlarging the kingdom.

You are a child of the King, an heir with Christ, and a person filled with the same Spirit that filled David at the moment of his anointing. You have within you the knowledge, skills, and abilities you need to face whatever is holding you back from God's plan.

You need to stop letting fear dictate your life while you claim to follow Christ. Reckless faith isn't stopped when fear presents itself. That's what faith is all about. Faith is choosing to move forward and accept God's plan even when you are scared to death.

David felt fear. He was human. The difference is that David didn't allow his fear to hold him back like everyone else on the battlefield that day. He moved forward knowing that God would be with him.

That is the word I want you to hear too. Move forward with confidence knowing that God will be with you. He won't leave you by yourself. God will give you the strength, wisdom, and authority you need to break through the barriers that fear and intimidation have placed in your life. Living free is empowering. That's the Good News Christians have been dying for since Jesus walked this earth.

Day 30

⌑

GOD WILL ALWAYS BE
FAITHFUL AND WILL ALWAYS
FOLLOW THROUGH

The life of David is an exciting one. He went from being the youngest of eight brothers to the most celebrated king in Israel's history. David left his mark not only in the history pages of his people, he also composed a songbook that has played a central part of the Christian faith since its inception: the book of Psalms.

David didn't always make good decisions. He didn't always follow God's plan. He actions weren't always consistent with someone who is described as being a man after God's heart. Nevertheless, David remained the most popular and well-liked king in Israel's history.

It was David who went on to lead the Israelites consistently to victory. It was David who ensured the temple would be built, even though it was his son, Solomon, who would oversee its construction. Even the genealogy of Jesus is traced to David in the gospels. Throughout the remainder of the Bible, David is characterized as someone who was blessed and favored by God.

As we look back on the life of David, we find evidence that God will always be faithful and will always follow through. Let me be clear: God's faithfulness doesn't mean we won't experience adversity, pain, and suffering. That is part of the human experience and was introduced into the world as a result of original sin. .

Until Christ returns, we will experience feelings of fear, intimidation, and defeat. What is most important to remember is that while those feelings exist, we are not captive to them. That means we don't have to let those feelings dictate the type of life that we will live.

That is a dangerous trap that we often find ourselves in. We look around and decide that facing what is holding us back is more effort than it's worth. We get tired in our own strength so we sit back and deal with what we know rather than pushing forward toward what God has planned for us.

If that is you today, you need to know that the Enemy wants you to think that the cost will be too much. He wants you to believe that what you know about life today is all you need to know. The Enemy never wants to make room for you to discover something as powerful as a breakthrough.

David was consistently underestimated, even by his own family. He was never given a fair shot, if you will. When Samuel came to visit, David was sent away to take care of the sheep. David had to deal with a dad who never saw the king in him, who never saw the potential in him. It took another man to recognize the king in him. When it was time for war, David was sent to take care of the house while his brothers fought. Later, he was asked to bring them food. When David decided to challenge Goliath, no one believed he would even survive.

Being underestimated isn't that bad. I was told I couldn't write, yet I'm writing this book. I was told I couldn't preach, yet I preach at one of the largest churches in Australia and have preached all over the world. I was told I was wasting my time and other people's money trying to start a political party that championed the family, yet we raised the money we needed and succeed at getting our first candidate elected.

I wonder in what ways have you been underestimated. Who has counted you out? Who thinks you're not up to the challenge? Who believes that you're not smart enough, good enough, or experienced enough to accomplish whatever dreams or vision God has given you?

> God will come through for you every time. You don't have to let fear and intimidation rule your life any longer.

I'm sorry you've had to endure people in your life who've told you no when God says yes. I have those people in my life too. If I'm not careful, they'll cause me to trip up and fall flat on my face.

I remember talking to an older man a number of years ago and he reminded me that he had been my seventh grade Sunday School teacher. He was obviously amazed at what I was doing now and he said to me: "I remember in my mind looking at you in seventh grade and predicting you as the person most likely to fail." I remember saying to him a bit cheekily, "Wow. I can't believe I had a Sunday School teacher with such incredible perception."

The Enemy uses those people to turn my attention away from the victory that has been sealed for me in Christ. In short, you have to stop listening to those people. Paul writes to the church at Corinth encouraging believers to "take captive every thought to make it obedient to Christ" (2 Cor. 10:5). Think, believe, and act may be an accurate description of how we shape and modify our behavior. It doesn't mean you have to act on every thought you have.

Your mind is a powerful tool. It shapes the way you view the world. Part of the plan to break through that I will outline in the next section of this book involves steps to stop your mind from carrying you away from the solid foundation of faith.

When you aren't sure if you can get up, know that God is faithful.

When you wonder if the pain will last forever, know that God is faithful.

When you question your faith and wonder if you heard God correctly, know that God is faithful.

God will come through for you every time. You don't have to let fear and intimidation rule your life any longer. You simply need to trust in the character of God rather than look at the circumstances of your life.

You can be free from the fear that is holding you back from God's plan.

Don't stop. Don't wait. Don't pause. Move forward with confidence and slay whatever Goliath is standing in your way.

If you think it's too big, remember God is with you.

If you think your opponent is too strong, remember God is with you.

If you think the risk is too great, remember God is with you.

God did not save you from the slavery of sin only to place you in the slavery of fear and intimidation. He saved you to set you free. That freedom is eternal and is not dependent upon anything but our obedience to follow Him.

Are you ready for the breakthrough God wants to give you?

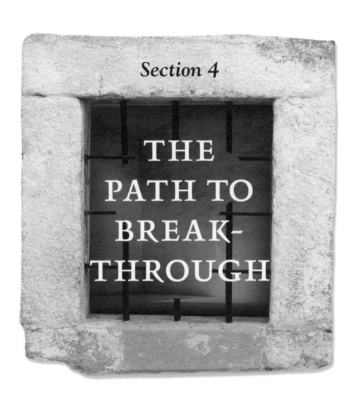

Section 4

THE PATH TO BREAK-THROUGH

Day 31

BELIEVE YOU WERE CREATED
TO ACCOMPLISH SOMETHING
OF SIGNIFICANCE

Congratulations on making it this far! We've covered some significant ground in the first three sections of this book. We've unpacked how fear and intimidation hold us back from what God wants for us. We've considered how authority gives us the power and confidence to accept God's blessing and multiply our influence. And we've reviewed how God, our Creator, designed us to make a difference in the world.

My guess is you wouldn't have read this far if you weren't connecting with what has been discussed. I'm not sure what your circumstances or life has been like up to this point. You may feel locked up, bound up, and held up by things that seem to be out of your control. You may feel like giving up (and perhaps you're on the verge of that now).

If that's you, then I have good news for you! The final section of the book will reveal the path to breakthrough. We're going to move from learning to implementation. The most important thing you can do to break free from the power fear and intimidation have on your life right now is to take a step forward.

Robert Frost once wrote, "The best way out is through." I believe that. The most difficult times often give us insight into life, faith, and people. Difficult times also sharpen us, make us stronger, and solidify our resolve to accept the blessing and favor that God intends to give us.

I told you a little about my burnout earlier in this book. It was a very dark time in my life. One of the challenges during that time was that I couldn't stop doing all the things that I normally do—like being a pastor, husband, father, son, etc. I still had things that were required of me. I didn't get to go away from everything, live on a resort, and be attended to by a team of psychologists and others helping me move toward recovery. (By the way, that treatment plan only happens in the movies.) My guess is that when you experience burnout, you don't get to check out either.

> **You should have confidence that whatever power fear and intimidation play in your life, the power God has placed within you, through the Holy Spirit, is greater.**

Just like you, I had to find my way through my burnout in the midst of still doing all the things that I was expected to do. If you feel like that's too much, let me encourage you with Jesus' words to His disciples who were feeling overwhelmed themselves. He says, "With man this is impossible, but with God all things are possible" (Matt. 19:26).

There are four things that I want you to do before we go any further: believe that you were created for a God-sized mission; acknowledge that fear and intimidation are holding you back; accept the authority you have in Christ; and trust that God is Who He says He is. Only if we are able to agree on these principles will the contents of these next pages make a difference in your lives. It's okay to wonder what freedom will feel like; it's not okay to wonder if freedom is even possible. We've already been made free in Christ.

You must believe that you were created for a God-sized mission. Your life has purpose and meaning. It may not feel like it. No one may have ever told you that before. God created you for a purpose and wants to do something through you that is unique and different and will change the world in a significant way.

You must acknowledge that fear and intimidation are holding you back. It's very difficult to overcome anything until you are willing to be honest with yourself and others. Fear works its way into our lives very subtly. Once it takes up residence in our minds, it begins to make its way into every nook and cranny until we are paralyzed and held captive to it. This is exactly where the Enemy wants you to be. It's the only way he can distract you from God's plan for your life. Be honest. Admit it. Say it out loud. This is the beginning of breaking free.

You must accept the authority you have in Christ. God has given you authority, dominion, and power because He wants to accomplish great things in and through you. You should have confidence that whatever power fear and intimidation play in your life, the power God has placed within you, through the Holy Spirit, is greater. The Bible says, "You, dear children, are from God and have overcome them, because the one who is in you is greater than the one who is in the world" (1 John 4:4).

You can break free. That's been God's plan all along.

You must trust that God is who He says He is. The Bible says God is the source of all life. He has a blueprint for your life, one that is full of blessing and divine favor. The Enemy also has a blueprint for your life, one that if full of fear and unmet expectations. You must recognize the contrast between a person who lives free in God's blessing and a person whose life is limited by fear and intimidation.

This may be how you feel right now. That's okay. I am writing this book because I've been there too. I've claimed the freedom I have in Christ, and it is possible for you to do the same.

I want you to promise me that you won't read too quickly through this last section. A good goal would be to read only one day's worth of reading at a time. If you try to read too much too quickly, you'll miss some of the growth that God wants to do in you. It would be no different than never running and then trying to run a marathon. When you try to do too much too quickly, you won't make it to the finish line before you give up and quit.

God has big things in store for you. This is only the beginning!

Day 32

·ᴛ—ᴛ·

DECIDE TO FACE
WHAT YOU FEAR THE MOST
WITH CONFIDENCE

The most significant step you can take in your path to breakthrough is to take decisive action. The scariest part of taking action is opening yourself up to the possibility of failure and success. You might succeed, but you also might fail.

This is exactly how fear works in your life. You feel God moving you in a certain direction, and then you are struck with the reality that God's plan might be out of reach—or even worse—impossible. When you feel like this, you can rest assured you have an important decision to make. Will you allow fear to hold you back, or will you accept the freedom you have been given in Christ?

Michael Jordan needs no introduction. You don't even have to be a sports fan to understand the significance of such an important athlete. He is arguably the most well-known and successful basketball player of all time.

Nike ran a very compelling commercial several years ago describing the substance of Michael Jordan's success. The script reads, "I've missed more than 9,000 shots in my career. I've lost almost 300 games. Twenty-six times I've been trusted to take the game winning shot and missed. I've failed over and over again in my life, and that's why I succeed." Isn't that true about life, too?

Failure is not what we should fear the most. It's our inability to step up to our fear with confidence that is much more dangerous and debilitating. Just recently, my son came home from school saying that he didn't want to try out for the math competition in case he didn't get the highest score. We had to realign his thinking so that he could confidently face the challenge and do his best regardless of the result. You might be convinced the worst thing in the world is to fail. I want to tell you that when you fail, you see God the clearest.

> *What failure does, however, is strip out the pretense in your life so you can see yourself for who you are and God for who He is.*

I'm not suggesting that God plans for you to fail. He doesn't want you to experience pain and suffering. That would be cruel and inconsistent with God's character.

The Enemy wants you to believe that what you will find is not pleasing. What God knows is that He created you and loves you. It's when we stop trying to be good enough and perfect that we begin to understand that we are God's beautiful creation, someone with value, purpose, and meaning.

When you believe that you are someone with value, purpose, and meaning, the limits in your mind are lifted and you begin to see what's possible, rather than the obstacles that stand in your way. Nothing has changed at this point. The challenges are still there. What will change is that you will begin to see life through God's eyes instead of the eyes of the Enemy.

This subtle change has already started to move you forward. The question is not if you can overcome and break free, but it is how are you going to do it. With that resolve, you are ready to decide to face what you fear the most with confidence.

Something powerful takes place when we decide to take action and take the first step forward. Fear doesn't seem as consuming, authority seems more believable, and God feels very present in that moment. Action is the pivot point by which you move from reacting to your limitations to acting on the limitless promises of God.

There are three things that will help you resolve to face your fear with confidence: speak your fear out loud, write down your fear, rethink your life without fear. As we've already explored earlier in this book, saying out loud what you fear the most makes it manageable. Next, writing your fear on paper and describing how it limits your life diminishes its power. Finally, rethinking your life without that fear helps you understand what effect freedom will have on your life.

Speak your fear out loud. Get in front of a mirror and say it to yourself. Find your spouse or close friend and tell them about it. You might also choose to gather a few close friends who have committed to walk through this with you and tell them too. This is the first step toward choosing another approach to life, one that accepts the authority you have been given in Christ.

Write down your fear. You don't have to be a literary genius or even own a computer. Do it the old-fashioned way. Find a piece of paper and a pencil and write your fear down. Describe how it is limiting your life. Try to be as specific as possible. Once you have written this down, go ahead and rethink your life without fear. Imagine what your life would be like if what you fear didn't control you. What would change in your life right now if you were no longer held back by this fear? How would your life change if whatever intimidates you went away?

This new life is possible, and God wants to give you exactly what your heart desires.

An important step toward recovery is beginning to imagine a new way of living. Let me encourage you now to put a red line through what you have just written, and then write out underneath this the new way of living you have just imagined. Make positive statements about how that would look. Now tape it up on your bathroom mirror or put it somewhere you'll see it regularly to constantly remind you of the journey you have embarked on.

The first step toward freedom begins with fully understanding what it is you're facing, limiting its power by saying it out loud and writing it down, and imaging a new way of living without that fear controlling you. This new life is possible, and God wants to give you exactly what your heart desires.

You may feel like I'm moving too slow. What I can tell you from experience is the decision to act, to reposition yourself for forward momentum, is the single most important step you can take right now to begin to break free from the fear and intimidation that is keeping you from realizing the blessings and experiencing the favor God wants to give you. Your new life begins right now. Are you ready?

Day 33

COMMIT TO ACHIEVING GOALS THAT FORCE YOU TO REACH FOR THE IMPOSSIBLE

I want to tell you something that you need to hear and understand. Every time you look for a breakthrough, you are going to feel uncomfortable, out of sorts, and even fearful. Everything will feel out of control.

You will feel things you never have before and it might make you anxious. Most people do not live free of fear and intimidation, so it only makes sense that as we move closer to breakthrough that we begin to feel different. The temptation you will have to fight is to lift your foot off the gas and allow your forward momentum to slow to a stop before you reach the point of breakthrough.

As you get closer and closer to God's plan for your life, the voice of intimidation becomes stronger with the hopes that you will back off. It's time to change that. It's time to look intimidation in the eye until it blinks because on the other side is freedom, liberation, and opportunity.

One of the ways you do that is to reach for goals you think are impossible to achieve. I'm not talking about leaping buildings in a single bound or moving faster than a speeding bullet. No one expects you to be superhuman, but God does call you to live a life that is full of abundance, power, and dominion.

If the faith of a mustard seed can move mountains, then you can do something unimaginable with your life too. Children dream big because they are not aware of any limits. It never occurs to a child how much money it will cost, what kind of education they'll need, or why it won't work. The impossible is always possible because there are no boundaries or limits.

Breakthrough is not safe. It's messy. It's full of ups and downs, and freedom from fear and intimidation doesn't necessarily mean that you'll see immediate results. Very often the biggest signs of progress are seen after months and months of consistently pushing forward. The cumulative effect is amazing, though. I have witnessed this first-hand in my own life. It has been the repetitive confrontation of intimidation that silenced it's voice over time. Every time I choose to actively confront how I feel and do the opposite, the chain gets weaker. I worked on the principle that if I practiced facing my fears, there would have to come a time when the fear would subside. It did for me and it will for you.

I want you to pull out a piece of paper. Write down the dreams you had about your life growing up. Maybe you wanted to be a teacher or an astronaut. Maybe you wanted to own your own business or drive a certain car. Maybe you wanted to graduate from college or go back to graduate school.

Somewhere along the way you gave up on those dreams. You thought they were too big and ultimately declared them impossible. You allowed the things that were holding you back to become reasons to stop moving forward.

Now I want you to list all the steps that need to take place for you to get from where you are today to making those dreams a reality. Don't edit yourself, even if some of the steps seem beyond unbelief. Try to list every step you'll need take to get there.

This is your game plan. You may say, "Ashley, this is impossible." If we were sitting across the table from one another, I would tell you that's when you know your reaching high enough to get close to what God has in mind for you.

The fallacy in our thinking is that we don't have the mind of God. Even our biggest dreams fall short of what God wants to do in and through us. I would never have thought God would have done all that He has through a poor, missionary kid. The life I had dreamed for myself moved me forward, but I never could have anticipated the transformation that took place in the process. As I moved forward, God redirected my attention toward the plan He had for me.

We can't escape God's plan, even when we reach for the impossible.

The path to breakthrough is not about using our minds to create the world that we want. It's recognizing that putting ourselves in situations that seem impossible is the only way to push through the boundaries we wrongly place on our thinking, believing, and acting. God did not save us to leave us where we are. He knows that growth does not happen when we are standing still.

The Enemy wants to do everything in his power to keep you from moving forward. He knows that if you begin to believe that the impossible is impossible, then you'll eventually stop reaching. Is that where you are today?

Do you believe that your marriage can't be repaired? Do you think going back to school to finish your degree is out of reach? Do you think changing careers is too risky?

Whatever dreams you listed, why did you give up? Who told you that it couldn't be done? What is keeping you from pursuing those dreams right now?

The truth is that nothing is keeping you from following your dreams. Even Jonah, who tried as hard as he could to run from God's plan, ran right into the presence of God. We can't escape God's plan, even when we reach for the impossible.

The steps you listed are goals. I want you to commit to finding a way to accomplish the next step. Wherever you are today, take the next step. Each step you take toward your next goal will build confidence and forward momentum. It may take you a lifetime, but God is so much more interested in the journey than the destination.

Commit to following this plan. Adjust when necessary. Only promise me that you won't give up. The temptation will be great. The arguments will seem logical. And strangely enough, people will try to deter you.

Paul tells us to, "run in such a way as to get the prize" (1 Cor. 9:24). God has not given up on you. He still wants to do great things through you. What God dreams for you, He will accomplish in you, as long as you don't continue to allow fear and intimidation to believe the impossible is out of reach.

Take the next step!

Day 34

BUILD A FORTRESS AROUND YOUR MIND TO PROTECT YOUR THINKING

Burnout is a difficult state of being. It's an odd and surreal feeling when the world around you is moving one hundred miles per second, too fast to even make sense of what is passing you by. It's a strange place to be.

I remember sitting on the front row of the church. I would think to myself in the moments leading up to the time I preached about how bad everything seemed. I told myself that the church was getting smaller, people were leaving, and it was over.

People needed to hear a word of hope from me. I knew that my preaching time was an opportunity to teach, encourage, and empower people to act on the authority and dominion that God had given them. It's a very difficult task to try to do those things yet fight the battle in your own mind.

In the middle of my inner ramblings, it occurred to me that if those things were true (and they were not), then what did I have to lose? I might as well say exactly what God had given me to say. I might as well act on the things I knew He was calling me to do. If everything was indeed falling apart, then what could my obedience do to stop it?

In that moment, I decided to preach exactly the message that God had given me to preach. His spirit was unleashed. Many people came to know the Lord that day, and I was reminded how important it was to build a fortress around my mind to protect my thinking. I did that every Sunday for months, and I began to declare over the church growth and increase, when everything inside me felt like it was decreasing.

> The secret of mind renewal doesn't start in your mind but with your eyes.

I want to share with you a very simple but profound thought about how to renew your mind. This will blow you away.

The truth is that the mind is only the processor. It is only the back office. The secret of mind renewal doesn't start in your mind but with your eyes. If you will just fill your eyes with pictures of the future and God's will for your life, your mind will renew itself.

We renew our minds by renewing our eyes. The Bible says, "The eye is the lamp of the body. If your eyes are good, your whole body will be full of light" (Matt 6:22). In the same way a lamp lights up a room so you can navigate your way through it, so your eyes brings information to your mind. Your eyes inform and influence your mind. Your eyes affect how you feel. Your eyes influence your desire. Your eyes influence your actions.

Our hearts were moved as we watched the television images of Australians in the bushfires in Victoria. When I heard about it, it sounded terrible. But when I saw people wandering around in a daze, homes burnt to the ground, distressed relatives who had lost loved ones, and people sleeping on mattresses next to hundreds of others in a community hall, it impacted me profoundly. I suddenly got emotional. It affected my thoughts and prompted me to give money. My eyes had powerfully impacted my thoughts, which in turn influenced my behavior.

Your eyes are like a camera. Your eyes take snapshots of your marriage, your boss, your finances, your health, and e-mail these images to your mind. This is your reality. You are afraid you're going to die, get divorced, become unemployed, or lose your kids.

Everyday your eyes are gathering information about your life. Everyday your eyes transmit to your brain, information about your reality. Based on the information your mind gets from your eyes, your mind either starts to worry, get upset, get depressed, feel discouraged, or gets elated, excited, and full of hope. The great struggle is to replace the negative pictures of your current reality with the faith pictures of God's will for your future.

My eyes are often bombarding my mind with the pictures of a negative reality. When it does, my mind stays fearful and faithless so I have to fight back. I have to start creating a picture of my future so that my mind is renewed and starts to believe.

Paul writes to the Christians in Ephesus:

I pray also that you may know him better that they eyes of your heart may be enlightened in order that you may know the hope to which he has called you, the riches of his glorious inheritance in the saints, and his incomparably great power for us who believe (Eph. 1:18–19).

The power of the eyes on the attitudes of the mind and the actions of the body is tangible.

Original sin came into the world through a thought that was conceived through the window of the eye. The Bible says, "When the woman saw that the fruit of the tree was good for food and pleasing to the eye, and also desirable for gaining wisdom, she took some and ate it" (Gen. 3:6). It was her eyes that affected everything else. Her eyes influenced her mind so powerfully that the desire to do wrong was overwhelming. Her eyes impacted what she believed and, ultimately, what she did.

Jesus says, "And if your eye causes you to sin, gouge it out and throw it away" (Matt. 18:9). Your eye has such power over your mind that if you look at the wrong thing, your mind will follow. The good news is that the opposite is also true. If you can just look at the right things, your mind will follow.

If you can influence your eyes, you can influence your mind. What you see, you'll be. What do you see when you look at your kids? What do you see when you look at your finances? What do you see when you look at your church? What do you see when you look at your ministry? What do you see when you look at your work? We did an exercise with our staff that proved to be very powerful. We asked them to find or create images to depict what they would like to see in each area of their lives: their relationships, their work, their ministry, their family, etc. Then we had everyone pass them around the staff room so that for weeks and weeks all they saw when they came into work were images of their future before them. The result was increased energy and enthusiasm as they began to feed their mind with those images.

Protecting your mind is very important. Your thinking shapes the way you see the world around you. It also informs you as to why certain things take place.

I want to ask you something. Has 'giving into fear ever made your quality of life any better? Of course not! It's made you feel oppressed, bound, tormented, and depressed.

The Bible says that we will have the victory, "not by might, nor by power," but by the spirit of God (Zech. 4:6). You must build a fortress around your mind to keep you from allowing fear and intimidation to control you. This is the best chance the Enemy has to keep you from living the life He has called you to live and being the person He has called you to be.

Protecting your mind is very important. Your thinking shapes the way you see the world around you.

There are four steps to protecting your mind: change your attitude; evaluate what you expose yourself to; surround yourself with people who will hold you accountable; and choose freedom. Let's unpack these. Following them will take you where you believe God is leading.

Change your attitude. Paul write to Timothy and says, "For God did not give us a spirit of timidity, but a spirit of power, of love, and of self-discipline" (2 Tim. 1:7). Stop allowing your mind to run free. Every part of our being is subject to God's authority. Fear confuses the Creator with His creation. If you are responsible, then your power is limited. If God is the source of our strength, then His power will never run out. Your attitude will enslave you or make you free. Which would you prefer?

Evaluate what you expose yourself to. This was something that I understood more clearly once Jane and I had children. What we watched and read and exposed ourselves to had to change to be age appropriate for our kids. We had to see things through the eyes of a child, as some of the things we watched had the potential to frighten them.

In much the same way, you must be diligent about what you watch, read, and expose yourself to. People, ideas, and environments influence your perspective. Don't expose yourself to things that are going to feed your fear.

Surround yourself with people who will hold you accountable. Nothing has been more powerful in experiencing breakthrough in my life than people who hold me accountable to my decisions, direction, and declarations. Once I had made a decision to face my fear and break the power of intimidation, I needed people around me who would hold me accountable to my decision and encourage me from retreating when the going got tough. People who would pull me up when my speech didn't match the faith declarations I had made earlier. This can be a challenging and vulnerable thing to do, but it's well worth it because you'll need support in your journey to freedom. Do you have people in your life who see through the pretense and hold you accountable?

Choose freedom. No one can be helped if they refuse to be helped. This is a key step in recovery for anyone struggling with addiction. It's easy to notice someone who is addicted to alcohol, drugs, or even sex. I am convinced that there is an addiction more subtle and stronger than any of those things. It is an addiction to fear. Many have become so dependent on fear that they've lost any sense of what life might be like without it. Freedom is what God wants for us. Why choose fear?

Day 35

——

MEDITATE
ON SCRIPTURE

Never underestimate the role Scripture plays in the path to breakthrough. We can read the most popular books, talk to world-renowned psychologists, and expose ourselves to the best insight and wisdom this world has to offer. None of it compares to what we find in Scripture.

The Gospel of John begins, "In the beginning was the Word, and the Word was with God, and the Word was God" (John 1:1). Just a few verses later, John writes, "The Word became flesh and made his dwelling among us" (John 1:14). I am convinced that if you are going to overcome the hold that fear and intimidation has on your life, Scripture will be central to finding your way to freedom.

It certainly was the circuit breaker and faith creator in me when I was trying to find answers to the incredible fear I experienced in my burnout. As I've shared before, I am a worrier by nature. I pride myself on being able to think my way out of problems. But after being physically ill with an infection raging in my body for twelve months and consistently working seventy to eighty hours a week, I collapsed. Suddenly, everything started to fall apart.

I became consumed with the fear of cancer. To be clear, I never personally had cancer. It was the fear of cancer that ruled my life. Now it was only part of the symptoms of my burnout and breakdown, but I could no longer just think positively and shake off those thoughts.

> **Anything less than total dependence upon the work of the Spirit in our lives falls short of God's intention.**

Fear and intimidation had firmly wrapped themselves around my mind and emotions. I started to experience panic attacks. I had three and decided I would do anything not to have another one ever again.

I began trying to think about what I might say to someone in my position if I were their counselor. I would tell them to find every Scripture on fear and start meditating on it until God gave them a word about His power over fear.

When that revelation comes, the power of fear will go. No one had wanted to counsel me, so I decided to counsel myself. It makes me laugh today, but it was the scariest and darkest time of my life. I knew it was kill or be killed, so I extracted every Scripture on fear and worry in the Bible and started to read these verses over and over again every day. I started to meditate on every one of those scriptures every day.

I have to say that I initially felt nothing. For weeks, I would read these scriptures hoping that the fear would go but nothing changed. In fact, it got discouraging and boring to read these scriptures every day over and over again, but the other options of giving up and the fear of not finding a way out kept me going. For twelve weeks, every day I persisted. Then one day as I was reading the Gospel of Matthew. Jesus poses the question, "Who of you by worrying can add a single hour to his life?" (Matt. 6:27).

As I read it, it felt like all the lights of a football field went on and my spirit was flooded with light. It was like I got hit in the head with a mallet. I suddenly saw the truth in the Scripture for the very first time. The Holy Spirit pushed it deep into my spirit, and I suddenly got it.

I had been using worry as a tool to keep myself ahead of the game. If I can worry about getting cancer long enough, I'll get it early. I now realized that worrying would not extend my life for even one hour. Wow! It blew me away. At the same time, the heaviness and fear just vanished. It has never come back. This is the power you can experience when the Word of God invades your life too.

As people of the Word, we believe that God's presence resides within us in the form of the Holy Spirit. We also believe that the Spirit is present in the reading and preaching of His Word. That's why theology alone fails to bring about spiritual transformation. Anything less than total dependence upon the work of the Spirit in our lives falls short of God's intention.

When we trust in the power of God's Word to reveal Himself to us, we begin to understand that Scripture is more than words on a page. Scripture is, in fact, the voice of God captured on paper. He has a message for us, and He intends for us to search the depths of its contents to find Him and find freedom forever.

The prophet Isaiah says to a broken country, "My word that goes out from my mouth: It will not return to me empty, but will accomplish what I desire and achieve the purpose for which I sent it" (Isa. 55:11). This passage becomes even more significant when we connect the idea of God sending His Word to His people when we read the beginning of the Gospel of John. God's Word came to His people through His prophets, through Jesus, and it comes to you by the power of the Holy Spirit in the pages of Scripture.

If the Bible is the Word of God, then we must find a way to become consumed with what we find within its pages. This is the function of meditation. I'm not talking about the meditation typically associated with Eastern religions. The purpose of meditation as they understand it is to empty their minds. Biblical meditation is intended to fill our minds with Scripture to the point that we are changed by it.

I want to give you five steps to developing a habit of meditating on Scripture as a means to overcome fear and intimidation. I do want to warn you. Anyone who spends a great deal of time in Scripture will be changed. You will be confronted with what you believe. You will be asked to make adjustments in your life. My guess is that if you've read this far, change is what you're looking for. Let's proceed with that assumption in place.

The first step in developing a habit of meditating on Scripture is to find a translation that you understand. There has never been a better time than the present for easier access to God's Word . We can find it in numerous translations, various applications for our computer, tablets, and smart phones. We can even purchase audio versions of people reading the Bible for us. There is little reason why you shouldn't have easy access to a version of Scripture you are comfortable reading on a regular basis.

The second step in developing a habit of mediating on Scripture is to establish a reading plan. I have included a number of Scripture references at the back of this book that specifically address fear and intimidation. You don't have to commit to reading the entire Bible from cover to cover in one year, but find a plan that works for you. We have a reading plan on our website at Influencers Church that you may find helpful to download. We also have short devotions that can be downloaded free on the same site. Jane and I take a particular Bible passage and spend about six or seven minutes discussing it and helping you to apply the truth in it to your life in a relevant and authentic way. . Having these tools and a plan will help you be consistent and guide you when you don't know what to read next.

The third step in developing a habit of meditating on Scripture is to choose one verse and commit it to memory. Everyone memorizes differently. Some people choose to write it down over and over again. Some people choose to recite it out loud. I've even known some to tape the verse to their car steering wheel or bathroom mirror, so they would be reminded of it on a regular basis. It really doesn't matter what method you use. There is something powerful about committing Scripture to memory. After a while it becomes part of you and becomes a weapon to fight the fear when it tries to intimidate you.

The fourth step in developing a habit of meditating on Scripture is to journal about what you're reading and learning. Grab a notebook of some sort, either paper or electronic, and begin to write down some of the thoughts you've had while reading God's Word. This is a great discipline to begin to see how God is molding and shaping you as a believer. Writing down what you're thinking will not only help you slow down long enough to let it sink in, but it will also allow you to go back over it when you feel discouraged and need to be reminded of your progress.

The fifth and final step in developing a habit of meditating on Scripture is to commit to doing it daily. When you give a portion of your day back to God, you remind yourself that your life is centered on eternal things, not the temporary things of this world. It will help you keep things in focus too.

Let's put it all together. When you get up in the morning, you read the suggested reading as guided by your plan using a translation that is comfortable for you. Then, you are reminded of a key verse each week that you want to memorize when you get in your car and find your reminder on your steering wheel. During the day, you focus on one word and find some time to pause and reflect on that one word for a few minutes. Last, you set aside some time before you go to bed to write down what you're learning and how God is moving in your life.

There is no greater catalyst to experiencing breakthrough than mediating on Scripture. It may feel awkward at first, but don't give up. The results are worth the effort to develop this important spiritual discipline.

Day 36

DEVELOP
A SELF-TALK ROUTINE

I t may seem strange to follow up a focus on Scripture meditation with
something like developing a self-talk routine. Self-talk alone won't
bring change on the inside, but you need to understand that once you
have saturated your heart, mind, and spirit with God's Word, you need to
realign your self-talk to agree with what you've read, rather than contra-
dict it!

I have no objection to the self-help movement. Many people have
been helped with this genre of literature, books, and materials. There is,
however, a point at which you can no longer help yourself. It is possible
to reach the end of your strength. If you are not careful, the fear of failing
to help yourself will put you back in the same loop that led you to be held
captive by fear and intimidation in the first place.

Self-talk can be a very powerful tool if it is in harmony with what
God's Word says about you. . Fear and intimidation in most cases start in

the mind. It starts with the words you hear others say and continues with the words you say to yourself. If you think back to the story of David and Goliath, you'll find out what a pivotal part words played in the fear and intimidation that had them paralyzed. The Bible says, "For forty days the Philistine came forward every morning and evening and took his stand" (1 Sam. 17:16). He taunted them with words, diminished their abilities and strength, and ridiculed their God. His words ate away at the fabric of everything they had ever believed they could trust and left them wrestling with fear. Before David ever picked up the first stone, Goliath was winning in a powerful way. He was holding back the army of God's chosen people with his words.

The first thing that happens when you decide to go up against intimidation will be the temptation to engage in conversations that are designed to break down what you thought you believed and question it to a point where it seems like a lie. Whether those conversations happen outwardly or inwardly, they are all designed for the same destructive purpose. That's why I talk to my church about the danger of engaging in criticism, negativity, and cynicism. You can kill people with your words. I see it happen all the time.

Why is this so significant? The battle of intimidation is a battle of words long before it is anything else. When you face your intimidation head on, your attitude will be attacked. Your actions will be attacked. Your lack of experience will be attacked. Your strength of mind will be attacked, just as it was for David and the Israelites.

The Enemy knows that if he can control your mind, then he has disabled your ability to resist him and the fear that comes with his presence. David had multiple conversations with people on his way to the battlefield. Each time, he was encouraged to quit, give up, throw in the towel. No one would have faulted David from walking away.

David knew something that the others didn't. He knew that Goliath was using words to control the minds of God's people. David also had something that the others didn't have. He had hours and hours alone with God on the hillsides looking after sheep. He had conversation after conversation where God had encouraged him, spoken to him, affirmed him through his words, and because the reserve he had inside of him outweighed anything that others were saying to him, he could resist the intimidation it brought. David had spent hours and hours writing songs from his self-talk that agreed with God's talk about him. More than just positive thinking and good self–talk, these words gave him the edge. He knew exactly who he was, and no giant could convince him otherwise! As a result, David could concentrate on the prize rather than the pressure.

The role of self-talk is to capture the attention of your mind before it is held captive by fear. When you find yourself being beaten up by circumstances, pressure, and other people, stop and recognize what is taking place. Expect resistance as you move forward, but remain consistent and committed to the path to freedom. The Enemy won't let you go without a fight, but he is going to lose. He knows it, but he doesn't want you to know it.

David ignored the attacks on his character. When you capture the attention of your mind before it is held captive, you can prevent the damage your intimidator is trying to do to you. The Enemy will always try to get you to question the fundamentals of what you believe about yourself and about God. This is where Scripture meditation becomes critical in application. When our minds are saturated with the Word of God, we know what is true and what isn't.

God knows you have to experience the victory over your mind before you can experience any other type of victory.

David talked up the victories rather than agree with Saul about his age. Remind yourself that this isn't the first time you've been under attack. In fact, anticipate being under attack at different times in your life. This way you will be prepared and know what to do when it happens.

Trace your steps through the other times you have been victorious over intimidation. This will give you the confidence that only comes from having been there and come out on the other side successful. Notice that Goliath initiates the conversation, but David talks back. He doesn't allow Goliath to win the battle of the conversation. He fires right back. This is what you need to do too. You need to talk back to your fear and state who you are and stand your ground. Don't agree with those intimidating and fearful thoughts.

Next, David attacked Goliath's vulnerability rather than think about his own inability. Goliath may, in fact, have been a horrible fighter. We know he wasn't too smart. He knew how to control peoples' minds, and he knew that his size brought sheer terror to many who saw him. The same is true about the intimidation that is trying to hold you back. However big, powerful, or forceful it seems, believe that your God is stronger. God knows you have to experience the victory over your mind before you can experience any other type of victory.

I don't want you to miss the power of developing a self-talk routine. When you feel you are under attack by fear and intimidation, walk yourself through the story of David and Goliath. You will quickly realize that what you fear the most isn't anything you should fear in the first place.

Let me leave you with one last word of encouragement. Jesus says to us, "I have told you these things, so that in me you may have peace. In this world you will have trouble. But take heart! I have overcome the world" (John 16:33).

Today, ask God to affirm you, and let Him tell you what He thinks about you. Write it down, rehearse it, let it become your self-talk for today and every day from now on.

Day 37

ENGAGE IN A HEALTHY ALTERNATIVE THAT DEMANDS YOUR ATTENTION

There is no better way to balance your efforts to overcome intimidation and fear in your life than to find a healthy alternative that demands your attention. Self-talk is a powerful engine that will move you forward, but sometimes changing your physical activity can greatly assists you in the process.

Often the medical world will prescribe medication to dull the anxiety that you are experiencing. Sometimes this may be a necessary intervention, but it's not a long-term solution. What starts small can become a new form of captivity. As a pastor, I can tell you that the power of addiction can fall on anyone, rich or poor, weak or powerful, young or old.

It's easy to think that altering our state of mind is an acceptable coping mechanism. My contention is that the risk is too great and the benefit too small. Of course, if the chemical is illegal then there is no question.

Breaking the law is not a path to overcoming fear and intimidation. In fact, it only complicates it.

I do want to talk about a way to alter your state of being that doesn't involve any chemicals, and it's totally legal: fasting. We don't talk much about it in church, but the Bible mentions the word numerous times. To our detriment as Christians, it is largely a forgotten practice that is relegated to a few rather than the masses.

Fasting by itself is not inherently spiritual. Its strength comes in moving your focus and attention toward God by denying your body something like food or water. Whether our fast is partial or complete is not as important as the purity of our motives in doing so.

Looking outside the Christian tradition, Islam—arguably the fastest growing religion on the planet—places fasting as a central discipline. Ramadan is a special month for Muslims. During this time, every Muslim that has reached puberty is required to fast for thirty days. They do eat one meal in the evening along with prayer, but nothing—food nor drink—are allowed from sunrise to sunset. There are a few exceptions, of course.

The purpose of the fast for Muslims is to help them focus their attention on spiritual matters instead of the desires of their bodies. They also believe it is a way to stay connected to their dependence upon God for food, health, and life. Muslims do not dismiss the spiritual discipline of fasting as many Christians do.

Engaging in a healthy activity like fasting that demands your attention not only prepares you for victory but also increases your tolerance for intimidation.

If Muslims can come together all over the world and pray to a god who is not alive, how much more can you and I come before a God who is alive? The Bible says, "And will not God bring about justice for his chosen ones, who cry out to him day and night? Will he keep putting them off? I tell you, he will see that they get justice, and quickly" (Luke 18:7).

Christians, have access to a living God. If you are struggling to feel God's power, to hear His voice, to know His presence, and you are in the grip of fear and intimidation, then can I encourage you to begin to fast? Friends, it's time to kill the intimidating spirit over our lives and live free.

Fasting does become spiritual when it is combined with prayer.

This is when it becomes the most powerful supernatural force I've ever experienced. Fasting is also powerful because it is a declaration of the Lordship of Jesus Christ. It is a statement that your commitment to Him is more important than food or drink. It really has nothing to do with what kind of fast you go on, it really has to do with the sacrifice you are making to bring your life under the control of Jesus Christ. Jesus said that in order to be a genuine disciple, you have to take up your cross and die to self. I can't think of a more tangible expression of dying to self than not eating.

Fasting is healthy. Not only does it give your digestive system a rest, but when you are waging war on the fear and intimidation, changing your physical experience can become a powerful path to breakthrough. Engaging in a healthy activity like fasting that demands your attention not only prepares you for victory but also increases your tolerance for intimidation. You'll be stronger and better prepared to face whatever it is that is intimidating you head on.

One of the reasons fasting is so powerful is that it literally denies your flesh and feeds your spirit. When that happens, your spirit and God's spirit in you have the strength to overcome your body and your soul. Because of that, it brings an ability to rise above the issues in your life that are controlling you. It builds in us an ability to overcome.

If you can fast, you can come against anything that wants to oppress you. It causes your spirit to rule your life. It brings discipline to your emotions and trains your mind to be focused on the promises of God.

Another benefit of fasting is that it often reveals where we are weak. When the Enemy wants to attack us, he will go after our weakness. In the midst of fasting, we discover those areas of our lives that leave room for fear and intimidation to become real. God gave us the discipline of fasting so that we would regularly realign our body soul and spirit into the order that best prepares us to fight intimidation.

Nothing gets you sensitive to Jesus and full of faith like fasting and prayer.

The secret to a life of freedom is faith. There is no quicker way to build your faith than to fast and pray. Fasting to me is like a faith growth hormone of the spirit. Nothing gets you sensitive to Jesus and full of faith like fasting and prayer. Together they form an exothermic reaction, a combination punch that just rocks the challenges of your life and breaks the chains that are holding you back.

Without prayer, fasting has personal benefits, but it's really just a weight loss program. It has no spiritual power. I also recommend water- or fluid-only fasts. I'm going to be controversial, and some of you won't like this statement, but I believe partial fasts, Daniel fasts, and the like are really for beginners to get a taste for fasting. For me personally, Things really start to happen when you do a fluids or water fast.

There are many great sources that deal with the practical side of fasting, but I'd like to explain why many people who have tried fasting and prayer don't experience breakthrough. The reason is simple. Fasting and prayer is a spiritual exercise. Fasting is letting go of the natural, and prayer is grabbing hold of the supernatural. This combination is lethal because it supercharges your faith. However, unless you clearly decide and create a line between what you are going to do and not going to do, then you'll break your fast by eating something you know you shouldn't, and then you'll feel guilty and lose confidence and boldness. Because fasting and prayer is about faith, a broken fast then becomes unfruitful. So I encourage people to make a clear line.

Make a decision before you start your fast to make it either water-only or fluids-only. I remember someone asking me about a fluid-only fast and jokingly saying, "what if I blend a steak into liquid form, is that okay?" to which I replied yes. That might surprise you, but the point of the fast is create a clear line of what you will and won't do so that you know clearly what is in and what is out. You'll be amazed at how clarity will assist you to fast and pray with power

As stated, Fasting increases your faith. You can tangibly feel your faith taking off particularly on day four through seven and beyond. It's just incredible. The other thing I've experienced many times now is that my sensitivity to God increases dramatically, particularly again when I reach past day three. It's just amazing.

Maybe you've never considered fasting before. I would encourage you to talk to your doctor or pastor before you start. Again, you are not more spiritual if your fast is a complete fast or a partial fast. The objective is to purify your mind and spirit and to increase your spiritual energy so that you are fully focused on the things of God and are prepared when the Enemy comes to oppress you.

A tip for fasting so that you create a healthy routine that includes prayer is to pray during the times you usually dedicate to eating. So, if breakfast takes you fifteen minutes, instead of eating spend fifteen minutes in prayer. If at lunch you take a half hour, pray for half hour instead. And at dinner, if it usually takes forty-five minutes, then use that time to pray instead.

What you'll find is that you supercharge your spirit, your faith, and your sensitivity to God. You'll discover when you pray, things will happen. This routine has helped thousands of people, including me, align my life with God's plan.

Fasting is one healthy activity that has eternal side effects. It may be that the path to breakthrough begins with fasting. Pray about it. Try it. Watch God mold you and strengthen you in the process. You will not be the same when you've finished than when you began.

Day 38

DON'T LISTEN TO
NEGATIVE PEOPLE

Earlier we looked at the fantastic story in the Bible where Jesus heals Jairus' daughter (Mark 5). On the way to the miracle, Jesus did some very decisive things in order to break the power of death over this twelve-year-old girl. The most important one was to make sure he removed negative influences from the situation as quickly as possible.

The Bible says Jesus only took Peter, James, and John with Him. I can imagine the conversation between Thomas and Jesus. Thomas says, "Jesus, I want to come and see this for myself." Jesus responds, "Well Thomas, you are a good man, and you are going to leave a mark behind, that is for sure. But today, could you go and order lunch? We really can't afford to take you along in your present state."

Maybe that's not exactly how the conversation unfolded. All I know is that Jesus decided to exclude Thomas. The second thing He did was kick all the skeptics out of Jairus's house. Why? Because an atmosphere of faith is hindered when negative people pollute the atmosphere with fear and negativity. In the end, that little girl was healed.

There is a good chance that someone told you along the way that you weren't good enough, smart enough, tall enough, skinny enough, or "whatever enough" to be accepted. Maybe you always wanted to be an athlete but never made the cut. Maybe you always wanted friends but seemed on the outside. Maybe you always wanted the job of your dreams but had to settle for the job that was available.

> That means no matter what other people have said about you or what you might think about yourself, you are a special and valuable person in the eyes of God.

Wherever you are in life, negative people seem to exist. Here is a surprise: They even exist in the church. If I had a nickel for every time someone said something hurtful or limiting to another believer, I'd be a very rich man. We're not supposed to be like that.

Paul writes to the Christians at Ephesus, "Be imitators of God, therefore, as dearly loved children and live a life of love, just as Christ loved us and gave himself up for us as a fragrant offering and sacrifice to God" (Eph. 5:1). Too many times we are anything but "fragrant" in our conversations with others. The Enemy wants to bring divisiveness into God's church with the hopes that we'll turn toward each other rather than stay focused on helping each other break free from the things that are holding us back from the blessing and favor of God.

I want you to know something: You are valuable to God. You may not think you are, but God loves you. He created you with you in mind. He wants to give you so much more than you already are and have. God wants to do a unique work in and through you that will bring about the kingdom of God on earth.

You may wonder what qualifies you to be such an important person to the Creator of the universe. That's a valid question. When Jesus came to earth, He spent time with the outcasts, the poor, the broken, the forgotten, and the overlooked. What frustrated the religious leaders is that Jesus focused His attention on the people they believed deserved the least amount of attention from the Son of God.

That means no matter what other people have said about you or what you might think about yourself, you are a special and valuable person in the eyes of God. It was for you that Jesus came to earth to complete God's plan of salvation and redemption.

What you need to understand today is that Jesus went through hell to give you amazing gifts. And with the powerful gifts of God came the ultimate gift—freedom. He didn't just die on the cross for your sin. He didn't just die on the cross for your sickness. He died on the cross as a gift for you and for me. When you invited Jesus into your life, you not only received the power of God to be His child but you also received abilities from God.

I want you to know something: You matter in the kingdom of God. You may be the lowest paid person at work. You may never have graduated from high school. You may live in a small house and drive a small car. You even feel alone and forgotten. The good news is that you are significant in the kingdom. God created you to accomplish His plan on earth. He needs you.

You may have never considered your divine purpose. Sometimes the power to battle against something isn't as strong when you don't completely understand what you're fighting for. God's plan is not dependent upon you, but God has designed a special role for you to play as He works out His redemption for humankind until Jesus' return.

God gives each of us a divine restlessness that guides us as we discover how we have been uniquely gifted to advance the kingdom. Did you know that you are gifted? Did you know that only you can accomplish the work God wants to do on this earth? Did you know that the Enemy knows this and fears your success?

I want you to know something: You are a success. It may be hard for you to think of yourself in that way. No matter what you've done or where you've been, the Bible says that in Christ all of us are made new. Paul writes to the Christians at Corinth: "Therefore, if anyone is in Christ, he is a new creation; the old has gone, the new has come!" (2 Cor. 5:17).

It is not an accident that God gave us baptism in water as a symbol of being washed clean. That means we have a fresh start. We have the opportunity to do life differently from this day forward. There is nothing that can hold us back from experiencing the blessing and favor of God. It is ours because of Jesus.

So what do you do with negative people in your life who want to hold you back? Not everyone fully understands what you know to be true. It doesn't excuse their negativity, but you shouldn't allow it to take greater authority in your life than what you know to be true about God's favorable view of you.

When you do encounter negative people, pray for them. God gives us these instructions in Luke 6:28, "Bless those who curse you, pray for those who mistreat you." I can tell you from personal experience that prayer changes you as much as it brings about change in other people. Over time, you will begin to see the people you have been praying for through the eyes of God.

In some cases you may need to separate yourself, if you can, from negative people who are constantly being critical, pointing out your faults, or putting you down. Take an inventory of the friendships that you have. Do you hang around with small-minded, negative-thinking, adverse-speaking people? If so, you need to intentionally begin to look for people who are positive and build up rather than tear down. Surround yourself with people who will positively influence your thoughts and actions.

Ask yourself these questions: *Will spending time with this person drag me down or lift me up? Will he or she make me want to be a better person?* That may sound a little self-absorbed, but you become like those you are spending the most time with. If your friends are positive and encouraging and free from negativity, then you will become like that too. You'll end up influencing others in the same way.

Negativity can become a tool of the Enemy. When you have a positive focus, it's easy to spot those who don't, and as a result you'll be more likely to notice other people in desperate need of a breakthrough. When you are able to see negativity not as a direct attack but a symptom of fear and intimidation, you can redirect those gripped by it toward the One who created them and has a plan for their life too.

Day 39

PUT YOURSELF WHERE FEAR
AND INTIMIDATION WILL
REVEAL THEMSELVES

Intimidation is all about rendering you useless. It wants to make you feel like you don't have anything to say. It wants you to believe you can't change anything.

Those who are controlled by intimidation struggle to see that they have something to contribute and that they matter. If intimidation had its way in your life, you would constantly feel defeated, stop trying, and eventually give up.

If you are a believer, it's time to reverse the curse and start to intimidate intimidation. I'm talking about moving from a defensive position to an offensive attack. When you become close to breakthrough, it becomes evident that you must indeed face the fear long enough and frequently enough that it no longer has any power in your life.

I want to challenge you to do something that may seem counter-intuitive.

Put yourself where fear and intimidation will reveal themselves. This is turning the table on the Enemy. This is acting on the authority that you know you possess in Christ. This is taunting fear until it reveals itself to be the illusion that it has been all along.

It's much the same as asking God for patience and then wondering why so many annoying people are bugging you! How can you develop a greater patience than what you already possess unless you are placed in a situation that demands more patience of you and an opportunity to grow? We never grow in patience without our patience being tested.

It's the same with breaking the power of fear and intimidation in your life. Freedom is not about being wary and avoiding intimidating people or circumstances from now on. It's about choosing to test out your newfound freedom and practice it by facing things that previously would have had you cowering or running for cover.

God wants to set you free so that you can experience life in all its abundance.

Start small and celebrate each victory. If there is something you have been avoiding or running from, make a decision today to face it head on. Take the offensive position, covered in prayer, and armed with God's Word, and see that thing bow down to the authority that you have been given through Jesus.

Don't avoid situations any longer that have threatened you in the past., You are no longer that person. You have had a revelation of God's authority. You now know that God has a plan for your life. You know that He has set you up to win in life and is with you and never leaves your side.

If you've been imprisoned by fear for any length of time, you immediately recognize when freedom is in your reach. I want you to know that God wants to set you free so that you can experience life in all its abundance. This was not an empty promise Jesus made, for God does not make promises that He doesn't keep.

There are three things you should know as you shift to the offensive against fear and intimidation: fear will try to confuse you; intimidation will increase; neither fear nor intimidation will outlast your resolve to persevere. You will be able to break through because Jesus has already broken up the stronghold that fear might have had on your life. It's gone forever!

Jesus already endured whatever fear and intimidation might come your way. Before His earthly ministry began, Jesus went on a fast for forty days to demonstrate the purity of His purpose and the substance of His resolve. He endured and was faithful. You, too, have the power to endure and be found faithful.

Fear will try to confuse you. When Jesus is led out into the desert for forty days to face temptation, the first temptation that He faces is turning stones into bread. Jesus is on a forty-day fast. This was a complete fast, so He is probably very hungry. When the Enemy comes, he tries to confuse Jesus. He wants Jesus to believe that food is the source of His strength. Jesus reminds him that any strength of the body does not compare with the strength of His spirit. Food would feed His body, but He will be hungry again.

The Enemy wants you to believe that your body is the center of your being. Not true. It is the Spirit that lives in you that gives you true life. When you face your fear, expect confusion. Lean on the disciplines you've learned of Scripture meditation, fasting, and protecting your mind. You will win in the end.

Intimidation will increase. The next temptation that Jesus faces involves throwing Himself down with the expectation that angels will preserve His life. The Enemy taunts Jesus. God would not let His own Son create His own death, would He? Jesus sees right through the Enemy's strategy and successfully resists the invitation to test God's power.

When you go on the offensive, expect the Enemy to turn up the heat. Things will seem more difficult at first. Events will take place that seem almost unbearable at times. Keep moving forward. Be excited! This is when you know you are close to breakthrough. James encourages us with this: "Consider it pure joy, my brothers, whenever you face trials of many kinds, because you know that the testing of your faith develops perseverance. Perseverance must finish its work so that you may be mature and complete, not lacking anything" (James 1:2-4 NIV 1984). Neither fear nor temptation will outlast your resolve to persevere.

Finally, the Enemy tries to entice Jesus by promising Him dominion over the entire earth, if He will bow down and worship him. He's offering

Jesus dominion, or control, in return for lordship. In other words, Jesus can control the earth under the lordship of Satan So many times we are tempted to compromise with fear in return for peace. If I compromise, I still get a certain amount of peace, but nowhere near the amount I'm entitled to through the authority and freedom I have as a child of God!

The Enemy wants us to believe that fear and intimidation are his to wield and operate He uses them to attempt to control us and keep us from acting in the authority God has given us to overcome all things. Our focus on this truth will eventually push aside the fear and intimidation. On the other side of breakthrough is the life that we've always wanted.

Some of you have been imprisoned so long that you don't even remember what freedom was like. You question whether you have the strength for battle, let alone a full frontal assault on the Enemy.

You need to recognize that such thinking is straight from the Enemy and is his attempt to keep you from standing on the promises of God. It's time you stop allowing fear and intimidation to keep you captive.

Don't live as a slave to fear when you have been set free. You are already victorious. Allow God to reveal himself to you afresh through His Word and in the person of Jesus. God's blessing and favor are yours for the taking.

If anyone is waiting, it is God who waits for us to accept the gift of freedom He has bought for us. It's not out of your reach. Push through. Endure. Break those chains, for they have no power over you. You are a child of God, and in the name of Jesus, you are free!

Day 40

PERSIST UNTIL YOU EXPERIENCE BREAKTHROUGH

Today is the last day of this journey. In a lot of ways, it is just the beginning of a new journey and a new life that is not limited or restricted anymore by fear and intimidation. It's a journey that will last for the rest of your life. Your journey will not be without fear and intimidation. Rather, it will be one that overcomes each attempt to enslave you again.

You'll have a confidence based in your authority, a power based in God's Word, and an assurance that God is with you in each battle you face. Each time you experience a victory—no matter how small—your growth will be visible. You'll feel stronger and have greater confidence to face the future and embrace all that God has planned for you.

You can probably feel the shackles begin to loosen in your life. You probably have more confidence right now than you've had in a long time. You're ready. You're prepared. You have a plan. You know what to anticipate.

The last step is to know that you must persist until you experience breakthrough. Too many people have stopped just short of freedom. What a sad commentary on a life God intended to live free!

Freedom is what God has wanted for you from the beginning of creation.

If this describes your life, it no longer has to. You were created to be free from fear and intimidation, and you can be. Freedom is what God has wanted for you from the beginning of creation.

There are three great reasons to persist: (1) because it's right; (2) because it's now a habit; and (3) because we know we will win.

God designed us to be victorious. In fact, we are made in His image. We not only have God's power within us to win; we also have His capacity for winning! When we choose a life of defeat because we are living at the mercy of fear and intimidation, we are not accurately reflecting the image of God in which we were made.

It's right for you to win.

It's natural for you to win.

You were created to win.

Anything else is wrong for you. It feels wrong, looks wrong, and brings only defeat and less than what you were promised. It's right, too, because when you gain freedom, you become part of God's plan to free the world. Did you know that?

We persist because it's now a habit. We've talked a lot about spiritual disciplines in the last section of this book. God gives you disciplines so that you know what to do when you don't know what to do. The longer you practice those disciplines, the more natural they will become. At first it may seems like an insurmountable challenge to fight back and face intimidation, but the more you do it the easier it becomes until one day you just find yourself doing it as habit, with little effort or thought.

Success always begets success. The more successful you are at combating fear and intimidation, the more confidence you will gain. That confidence (not arrogance) will shape your resolve moving forward.

We persist because we know we will win. If I haven't been clear to this point, let me say it again: God has already won the victory, and it's yours to receive. It is your responsibility to accept the authority, dominion, and power He has given to you. When you know that the victory is yours, you will react like David did. He gave no consideration for any of the reasons why he shouldn't face Goliath. Instead, he ran toward the battle line and did the impossible. You can do that too.

Remember the story I told you about the bears who had lived in captivity their entire lives? When it was time for them to be released back into the wild, they were unsure of themselves. An environment that was supposed to be natural for them seemed scary, odd, and anything but normal.

You might be like that bear. You have been this way for so long, and over these forty days something has started to change. It's now time to persist and keep persisting until you find yourself forever free from the cage of fear and intimidation.

I can say from personal experience that there is a world of freedom waiting for you. It's a world that may feel uncomfortable for a while, but if you persist and keep persisting, you will start to live in the freedom that God intended for your life.

Do it for yourself. Do it for the Lord. Do it for the generations that will follow and for the people who are watching you are drawing their inspiration from your life. Do it for them and be amazed at what God does.

You are not alone in your journey. The Bible says, "Do not be afraid or terrified because of them, for the Lord your God goes with you; he will never leave you nor forsake you" (Deut. 31:6).

When I find myself in the midst of a battle for my freedom, I often visit Hebrews 11, which is sometimes called the Hall of Faith. This particular section of Scripture highlights not only the victory that God gives His children but also those who choose to believe and continue believing until they, too, experienced breakthrough.

As the writer of Hebrews brings this section to a close, he begins the next chapter with these words of affirmation, "Therefore, since we are surrounded by such a great cloud of witnesses, let us throw off everything that hinders and the sin that so easily entangles, and let us run with perseverance the race marked out for us" (Heb. 12:1). Fear and intimidation may be part of a fallen world, but they don't have to hold you back.

When you persist, you carry on the tradition of Christ, who persisted in the redemption of the world through the cross and resurrection. When you persist, you carry on the tradition of the martyrs who courageously died in the name of freedom. When you persist, you become God's witness to a world that has yet to realize the freedom you now know to be true.

You are free. With your freedom, you now carry on the responsibility to be vigilant in maintaining your freedom and in bringing about freedom in the lives of others. God designed you to multiply. May your life multiply the effects of freedom that the world may know God's favor and blessing is also available to them. As Jesus said, "If you hold to my teaching, you are really my disciples. Then you will know the truth, and the truth will set you free (John 8:31–32).

Become a freedom campaigner. Use the freedom you have found to help others find the freedom you now have. Because you have lived with fear, you can recognize it in the lives of others, so lead them gently to freedom and encourage them to do the same for others.

CONCLUSION

I f you just finished reading Day 40, congratulations! You made it! You're not just a survivor—you're a *thriver!*

Forty days is a significant number. Most psychologists believe habits are unlearned and new habits are formed within forty days. Forty is also a significant number in the Bible: the children of Israel wandered in the desert for forty years; the rain came as God had promised Noah for forty days and nights; and Jesus was tempted at the beginning of His ministry for forty days.

You shouldn't take your resolve to start and finish this process lightly. Something within you jumped at the chance to break free of whatever it is that was holding you back. You probably couldn't explain it when you started, but I bet you have a good idea what it is now. The spirit of God was stirring your heart and increased your desire for the freedom you have already been given in Christ.

By choosing to read through this book in forty days, there is a good chance that you've already started to see and experience new life as the grip of fear and intimidation has been loosened. Your new life has already begun!

Jesus once encountered a small group of lepers. Leprosy was a fatal disease in Jesus' day. It would eat your skin away. When someone was found to have leprosy, they were declared unclean. Worse, they had to leave everything behind immediately—their families, friends, jobs, and previous life—to go live just outside the city where others with the same disease lived together.

It was a brutal and immediate separation from life as it was meant to be experienced. When a leper would approach someone—even from a far distance—they were supposed to announce themselves and that they had leprosy. This is exactly what they did to Jesus as He came close to them.

I would imagine people who endured this horrible disease eventually became numb to the reaction of other people who were often terrified of contracting the disease themselves. Jesus acted differently. He spoke to them directly and healed them.

Before someone could be declared healed, a priest would have to inspect their body and officially declare them healed. These lepers ran straight to the priest to do just that. I don't blame them, do you? I would probably do the same thing.

One of the ten lepers whom Jesus had healed came back after being declared healed by the priest to thank Jesus. His response was profound. Jesus says, "Rise and go; your faith has made you well" (Luke 17:19).

Fear and intimidation are not much different from leprosy. It may not eat away at your flesh and result in disfigurement. However, it does consume your life to the point where it's hard to recognize the person you once were.

Jesus offers you freedom today. You have been healed because Jesus overcame death and the grave. Because He is alive in you, you have the authority, power, and dominion to do great things.

You must rise up. God is not done with you yet. Until He comes back in all His glory and this world passes away, you have an assignment to accomplish. It's not an option to sit on the sidelines waiting for Jesus to come back. Rise up. Get ready. God has big plans for your life.

You must go. God didn't save you so you could sit comfortably in your chair. He saved you so you could continue to spread the Good News. If you have experienced breakthrough then He has given you something to tell others about. Show them with your life what it means to live free. Tell those who ask that you have been healed, put back together, and been made new in Christ.

Remember, it is your faith that made you well. It is too easy to forget

God when we break away from fear. For a brief moment, you might be intoxicated with the new sense of freedom that you have. Just don't allow yourself to think that you had the power all along. The Enemy—who just lost—is trying to make a Hail Mary pass before the buzzer sounds and eternity is set in motion, but it won't work.

Your faith has made you well.

Your faith will carry you through.

Your faith overcomes.

I want you to know that today is the beginning of a change in your life. You have broken the chains of fear and intimidation. You have been liberated. This is cause for celebration!

Let your personality shine through with boldness and confidence. I want your potential to be unleashed so you can take possession of everything Jesus died to give you.

Your friends, your peers, your co-workers, your children, and your spouse are waiting to see that spark of life that they haven't seen in some time. They are waiting to feel the passion felt in the pace of your steps. They are waiting to sense the spirit of God moving in your life.

God is not done with you yet. Your work is not finished.

The prophet Isaiah says, "Those who hope in the Lord will renew their strength. They will soar on wings like eagles; they will run and not grow weary, they will walk and not be faint" (Isa. 40:31). That is a description of what a life looks like that is not bound by fear and intimidation. I want this for you. God wants this for you. You should want it for yourself because it is already yours.

Your new life—one of no more fear—begins now!

DISCUSSION QUESTIONS

SECTION 1—THE TRUTH ABOUT FEAR

1. What fears are you focusing on that prevent you from believing that what will be tomorrow is greater than what is today?

2. When was the last time you put yourself in a situation that forced you to take true risk? How would your life change if fear no longer held you back from following your heart, passions, and dreams?

3. Believers are taught to "seek first his kingdom" (Matt. 6:33). What happens when you take your focus off of Christ's kingdom? What do you value more: your stability or your obedience to the call of God on your life?

4. When in your life has discontent and complaining grown from a fear that your dreams might actually come true? Which of your biggest dreams does God want to turn into reality?

5. What point in your life did you stop believing in yourself—or at least the possibility of seeing your biggest dream come true? Was it after you graduated, when you settled into your career, got married, started having children, or just fell into a predictable routine?

6. Which of your fears stem from comparing yourself to others? How will turning your focus on God—the source of your blessing, anointing, and power—bring you freedom?

7. Fear keeps us from considering new approaches to our same problems. What things do you keep doing over and over in your life that hinder you from experiencing something new?

8. John writes, "You, dear children, are from God and have overcome them, because the one who is in you is greater than the one who is in the world" (1 John 4:4). Why does the impossibility of perfection control your life more than your perfect, limitless God?

9. Do you believe God limits extraordinary living? How have you been unwilling to believe in God's power and accept His blessing?

10. There is something liberating about saying what you fear out loud. What is it? If you can, tell it to someone else who can encourage you. At the very least, say it out loud to yourself.

SECTION 2—THE TRUTH ABOUT AUTHORITY

1. God has given you permission to have authority over fear. In what ways are you held captive to fear and intimidation instead of choosing to accept your God-given authority?

2. Jesus said, "I tell you the truth, anyone who has faith in me will do what I have been doing. He will do even greater things" (John 14:12). What is that first, big, scary step you need to take toward the direction God is calling you?

3. As a child of God, you are able to overcome "because the one who is in you is greater than the one who is in the world" (1 John 4:4). How is the Enemy attempting to reduce the size of your influence or diminish your dominion over specific areas of your life?

4. Read the following passage: Luke 4:32; Mark 1:27; Matthew 9:6–7; and Matthew 26:18. How do these accounts of the authority of Jesus impact your life?

5. When has "positive thinking" alone let you down? Why is that? How can you be better prepared to exercise your God-given authority when adversity comes?

6. What doors does God want open for you, if only you will believe in the authority that He has already placed within you? In what circumstances were you reminded that He alone is the source of your victory and authority?

7. What does God want to do through you?, What is standing in your way from claiming your rightful place and position of authority today?

8. Authority gives you clarity, discernment, and confidence, which are necessary to claim the full, abundant life you crave in your soul. What clarity have you received reading this chapter? What next step has discernment revealed to you? What confidence has God given you to courageously make a move?

9. King Nahash was willing to leave the Israelites alone if they allowed him to gouge out everyone's right eye (see 1 Sam. 11:2). Has fear made you accept a similar compromise? Instead of living in the victory that is clearly yours, how are you settling for only half of your inheritance as a child of God?

10. When do you feel like giving up? When is your road most difficult to travel? What dark times have you recently experienced? Explain how authority is key to your process of overcoming whatever is trying to keep you from the life God wants for you.

SECTION 3—THE TRUTH ABOUT GOD

1. How is your life like that of Saul's? God wanted Saul to be king, but that didn't happen because Saul tried to do things on his own. In what ways have you rejected God's plan for your life and forfeited His blessings?

2. It's hard to believe now that David was an unlikely candidate to become king. Why do you—or others, perhaps—not believe that God can use you in great ways? How does He want to multiply your life and use you to accomplish more than you ever thought possible?

3. A prophet of God may not have come to your house and poured oil over your head, but God has chosen you. Have you ever considered yourself anointed by God? What times in your life did you believe that God chose you for something special?

4. Which of your past decisions do you believe are keeping you from experiencing the future God wants to give you? What personal examples have proven to you that the God of the Bible is a God of second chances?

5. What are you facing today that has you paralyzed with fear? How has God taken you to the very edge in order for you to fully understand that your life is completely and securely in His hands?

6. A common theme in David's life is that he is consistently underestimated by others, yet he never hesitates and his conviction leads him to action. What skepticism or discouragement from others is holding you back?

7. What God-given talents and gifts has God given you? How are you using them to bring Him glory? What unique circumstances has God placed you in? How can you use these talents, gifts, and experiences to expand His kingdom?

8. What is standing in the way of you accepting the power and authority God wants to give you? Why do you believe or doubt that God is waiting to grant you victory over the Goliath in your life?

9. Enlarging the kingdom is about showing others there is another way to live. When you break free from the bondage of fear and choose to live out God's plan for your life, how will you influence the people around you?

10. Do you feel that you're not smart enough, good enough, or experienced enough to accomplish whatever dreams or vision God has given you? Has someone counted you out? What does God's faithfulness mean to you when (not if) you experience adversity, pain, and suffering?

SECTION 4—THE PATH TO BREAKTHROUGH

1. Do you believe that you were created for a God-sized mission? Can you acknowledge that fear and intimidation are holding you back? Have you accepted the authority you have in Christ? Do you trust that God is Who He says He is? Pray through these questions until you can answer each one of them with a yes.

2. The question is not if you can overcome and break free, but how you are going to do it. Do you believe that you are someone with value, purpose, and meaning? Why or why not? What do you need to do to see the possibilities on the other side of the obstacles?

3. What did you write down as the dreams you had growing up? What necessary steps do you need to take to make those dreams a reality?

4. You can experience victory "not by might, nor by power" but by the spirit of God (Zech. 4:6). Where do you need God to build a fortress around your mind in order to keep fear and intimidation from controlling you?

5. When is the last time you meditated on Scripture? Don't just read the Bible, but take a passage and let it consume you. And stick with it, even though it may feel awkward at first.

6. God knows you have to experience the victory over your mind before you can experience any other type of victory. What self-talk do you need to change to move you forward?

7. When was the last time you fasted? How did it give you the ability to rise above the issues in your life that were controlling you? How did it bring discipline to your emotions and train your mind to be focused on the promises of God? If you have never fasted, make a plan to start today.

8. Who are the negative people in your life? Pray for them now. And often. How does praying for these people change you, regardless of whether it changes them?

9. What intimidation do you need get rid of? How can you live according to the hope you have been given? God's blessing and favor is not just "up for grabs" but is waiting to be distributed. What is keeping you from believing that completely?

10. What do you need to do in order to persist beyond these forty days? Will you persist because it's right? Will you persist out of habit? Or will you persist because you know that you will win?

SCRIPTURE GUIDE
FOR PERSONAL DEVOTION

Genesis 15:1	After this, the word of the LORD came to Abram in a vision: "Do not be afraid, Abram. I am your shield, your very great reward."
Genesis 26:24	That night the LORD appeared to him and said, "I am the God of your father Abraham. Do not be afraid, for I am with you; I will bless you and will increase the number of your descendants for the sake of my servant Abraham."
Exodus 14:13	Moses answered the people, "Do not be afraid. Stand firm and you will see the deliverance the LORD will bring you today. The Egyptians you see today you will never see again.
Leviticus 26:6	"'I will grant peace in the land, and you will lie down and no one will make you afraid. I will remove savage beasts from the land, and the sword will not pass through your country.'"
Numbers 14:9	"Only do not rebel against the LORD. And do not be afraid of the people of the land, because we will swallow them up. Their protection is gone, but the LORD is with us. Do not be afraid of them."
Numbers 21:34	The LORD said to Moses, "Do not be afraid of him, for I have handed him over to you, with his whole army and his land. Do to him what you did to Sihon king of the Amorites, who reigned in Heshbon."
Deuteronomy 1:17	Do not show partiality in judging; hear both small and great alike. Do not be afraid of any man, for judgment belongs to God. Bring me any case too hard for you, and I will hear it.

Deuteronomy 1:21	See, the LORD your God has given you the land. Go up and take possession of it as the LORD, the God of your fathers, told you. Do not be afraid; do not be discouraged.
Deuteronomy 1:29	Then I said to you, "Do not be terrified; do not be afraid of them."
Deuteronomy 3:2	The LORD said to me, "Do not be afraid of him, for I have handed him over to you with his whole army and his land. Do to him what you did to Sihon king of the Amorites, who reigned in Heshbon."
Deuteronomy 3:22	Do not be afraid of them; the LORD your God himself will fight for you.
Deuteronomy 7:18	But do not be afraid of them; remember well what the LORD your God did to Pharaoh and to all Egypt.
Deuteronomy 20:1	When you go to war against your enemies and see horses and chariots and an army greater than yours, do not be afraid of them, because the LORD your God, who brought you up out of Egypt, will be with you.
Deuteronomy 20:3	He shall say: "Hear, O Israel, today you are going into battle against your enemies. Do not be fainthearted or afraid; do not be terrified or give way to panic before them."
Deuteronomy 31:6	"Be strong and courageous. Do not be afraid or terrified because of them, for the LORD your God goes with you; he will never leave you nor forsake you."
Deuteronomy 31:8	"The LORD himself goes before you and will be with you; he will never leave you nor forsake you. Do not be afraid; do not be discouraged."
Deuteronomy 33:27	The eternal God is your refuge, and underneath are the everlasting arms.
Joshua 8:1	Then the LORD said to Joshua, "Do not be afraid; do not be discouraged. Take the whole army with you, and go up and attack Ai. For I have delivered into your hands the king of Ai, his people, his city and his land."
Joshua 10:8	The LORD said to Joshua, "Do not be afraid of them; I have given them into your hand. Not one of them will be able to withstand you."
Joshua 10:25	Joshua said to them, "Do not be afraid; do not be discouraged. Be strong and courageous. This is what the LORD will do to all the enemies you are going to fight."

Joshua 11:6	The LORD said to Joshua, "Do not be afraid of them, because by this time tomorrow I will hand all of them over to Israel, slain. You are to hamstring their horses and burn their chariots."
Judges 6:23	But the LORD said to him, "Peace! Do not be afraid. You are not going to die."
Ruth 3:11	And now, my daughter, don't be afraid. I will do for you all you ask. All my fellow townsmen know that you are a woman of noble character.
1 Samuel 17:45	David said to the Philistine, "You come against me with sword and spear and javelin, but I come against you in the name of the Lord Almighty, the God of the armies of Israel, whom you have defied."
1 Samuel 22:23	Stay with me; don't be afraid; the man who is seeking your life is seeking mine also. You will be safe with me."
2 Samuel 13:28	Absalom ordered his men, "Listen! When Amnon is in high spirits from drinking wine and I say to you, 'Strike Amnon down,' then kill him. Don't be afraid. Have not I given you this order? Be strong and brave."
2 Kings 6:16	"Don't be afraid," the prophet answered. "Those who are with us are more than those who are with them."
2 Kings 19:6	Isaiah said to them, "Tell your master, 'This is what the LORD says: Do not be afraid of what you have heard— those words with which the underlings of the king of Assyria have blasphemed me.'"
1 Chronicles 22:13	Then you will have success if you are careful to observe the decrees and laws that the LORD gave Moses for Israel. Be strong and courageous. Do not be afraid or discouraged.
1 Chronicles 28:20	David also said to Solomon his son, "Be strong and courageous, and do the work. Do not be afraid or discouraged, for the LORD God, my God, is with you. He will not fail you or forsake you until all the work for the service of the temple of the LORD is finished."
2 Chronicles 20:15	He said: "Listen, King Jehoshaphat and all who live in Judah and Jerusalem! This is what the LORD says to you: 'Do not be afraid or discouraged because of this vast army. For the battle is not yours, but God's.'"

2 Chronicles 20:17	"'You will not have to fight this battle. Take up your positions; stand firm and see the deliverance the LORD will give you, O Judah and Jerusalem. Do not be afraid; do not be discouraged. Go out to face them tomorrow, and the LORD will be with you.'"
2 Chronicles 32:7	"Be strong and courageous. Do not be afraid or discouraged because of the king of Assyria and the vast army with him, for there is a greater power with us than with him."
Job 5:11	The lowly he sets on high, and those who mourn are lifted to safety.
Job 11:16	You will forget your misery; you will remember it as waters that have passed away.
Job 11:18	You will be secure, because there is hope; you will look about you and take your rest in safety.
Job 11:19	You will lie down, with no one to make you afraid, and many will court your favor.
Job 39:22	He laughs at fear, afraid of nothing; he does not shy away from the sword.
Psalm 4:8	I will lie down and sleep in peace, for you alone, O Lord, make me dwell in safety.
Psalm 16:8	I have set the Lord always before me. Because he is at my right hand, I will not be shaken.
Psalm 27:1	The LORD is my light and my salvation—whom shall I fear? The LORD is the stronghold of my life—of whom shall I be afraid?
Psalm 27:1, 3	The Lord is my light and my salvation; whom shall I fear? The Lord is the stronghold of my life; of whom shall I be afraid? Though an army encamp against me, my heart shall not fear; though war rise up against me, yet I will be confident.
Psalm 29:11	The Lord gives strength to his people; the Lord blesses his people with peace.
Psalm 32:7–8	You are my hiding place; you will protect me from trouble and surround me with songs of deliverance.
Psalm 34:4	I sought the Lord, and he answered me, and delivered me from all my fears.

Psalm 56:3	When I am afraid, I will trust in you.
Psalm 56:4	In God, whose word I praise, in God I trust; I will not be afraid. What can mortal man do to me?
Psalm 56:11	in God I trust; I will not be afraid. What can man do to me?
Psalm 62:1–2	My soul finds rest in God alone; my salvation comes from him. He alone is my rock and my salvation; he is my fortress, I will never be shaken.
Psalm 85:8	I will listen to what God the Lord will say; he promises peace to his people, his saints— but let them not return to folly.
Psalm 118:6	The LORD is with me; I will not be afraid. What can man do to me?
Psalm 121:10	Let the wicked fall into their own nets, while I pass by in safety.
Psalm 122:7	May there be peace within your walls and security within your citadels.
Psalm 138:3	When I called, you answered me; you made me bold and stouthearted.
Psalm 145:18–19	The Lord is near to all who call on him, to all who call on him in truth. He fulfills the desires of those who fear him; he hears their cry and saves them.
Psalm 147:14	He grants peace to your borders and satisfies you with the finest of wheat.
Proverbs 1:33	But whoever listens to me will live in safety and be at ease, without fear of harm.
Proverbs 3:5–6	Trust in the Lord with all your heart and lean not on your own understanding; in all your ways acknowledge him, and he will make your paths straight.
Proverbs 3:23	Then you will go on your way in safety, and your foot will not stumble.
Proverbs 3:24	when you lie down, you will not be afraid; when you lie down, your sleep will be sweet.
Proverbs 14:30	A heart at peace gives life to the body, but envy rots the bones.

Proverbs 18:10	The name of the Lord is a strong tower; the righteous run into it and are safe.
Proverbs 29:25	Fear of others will prove to be a snare, but whoever trusts in the Lord is kept safe.
Isaiah 7:4	Say to him, "Be careful, keep calm and don't be afraid. Do not lose heart because of these two smoldering stubs of firewood—because of the fierce anger of Rezin and Aram and of the son of Remaliah."
Isaiah 12:2	Surely God is my salvation; I will trust and not be afraid. The LORD, the LORD, is my strength and my song; he has become my salvation.
Isaiah 26:3–4	Those of steadfast mind you keep in peace—because they trust in you. Trust in the Lord forever, for in the Lord God you have an everlasting rock.
Isaiah 26:12	Lord, you establish peace for us; all that we have accomplished you have done for us.
Isaiah 32:17	The fruit of righteousness will be peace; the effect of righteousness will be quietness and confidence forever.
Isaiah 32:18	My people will live in peaceful dwelling places, in secure homes, in undisturbed places of rest.
Isaiah 37:6	Isaiah said to them, "Tell your master, 'This is what the LORD says: Do not be afraid of what you have heard—those words with which the underlings of the king of Assyria have blasphemed me.'"
Isaiah 40:9	You who bring good tidings to Zion, go up on a high mountain. You who bring good tidings to Jerusalem, lift up your voice with a shout, lift it up, do not be afraid; say to the towns of Judah, "Here is your God!"
Isaiah 41:10	So do not fear, for I am with you; do not be dismayed, for I am your God. I will strengthen you and help you; I will uphold you with my righteous right hand.
Isaiah 41:14	"Do not be afraid, O worm Jacob, O little Israel, for I myself will help you," declares the LORD, your Redeemer, the Holy One of Israel.
Isaiah 43:5	Do not be afraid, for I am with you; I will bring your children from the east and gather you from the west.

Isaiah 44:2	This is what the LORD says—"he who made you, who formed you in the womb, and who will help you: Do not be afraid, O Jacob, my servant, Jeshurun, whom I have chosen."
Isaiah 44:8	Do not tremble, do not be afraid. Did I not proclaim this and foretell it long ago? You are my witnesses. Is there any God besides me? No, there is no other Rock; I know not one.
Isaiah 54:4	"Do not be afraid; you will not suffer shame. Do not fear disgrace; you will not be humiliated. You will forget the shame of your youth and remember no more the reproach of your widowhood."
Jeremiah 1:8	"Do not be afraid of them, for I am with you and will rescue you," declares the LORD.
Jeremiah 16:19	O Lord, my strength and my fortress, my refuge in time of distress.
Jeremiah 17:8	He will be like a tree planted by the water that sends out its roots by the stream. It does not fear when heat comes; its leaves are always green. It has no worries in a year of drought and never fails to bear fruit.
Jeremiah 23:4	"I will place shepherds over them who will tend them, and they will no longer be afraid or terrified, nor will any be missing," declares the LORD.
Jeremiah 30:10	"So do not fear, O Jacob my servant; do not be dismayed, O Israel," declares the LORD. "I will surely save you out of a distant place, your descendants from the land of their exile. Jacob will again have peace and security, and no one will make him afraid."
Jeremiah 33:6	"Nevertheless, I will bring health and healing to it; I will heal my people and will let them enjoy abundant peace and security."
Jeremiah 42:11	"Do not be afraid of the king of Babylon, whom you now fear. Do not be afraid of him," declares the LORD, "for I am with you and will save you and deliver you from his hands."

Jeremiah 46:27	Do not fear, O Jacob my servant; do not be dismayed, O Israel. I will surely save you out of a distant place, your descendants from the land of their exile. Jacob will again have peace and security, and no one will make him afraid.
Jeremiah 51:46	Do not lose heart or be afraid when rumors are heard in the land; one rumor comes this year, another the next, rumors of violence in the land and of ruler against ruler.
Ezekiel 2:6	And you, son of man, do not be afraid of them or their words. Do not be afraid, though briers and thorns are all around you and you live among scorpions. Do not be afraid of what they say or terrified by them, though they are a rebellious house.
Ezekiel 34:28	They will no longer be plundered by the nations, nor will wild animals devour them. They will live in safety, and no one will make them afraid.
Ezekiel 39:26	They will forget their shame and all the unfaithfulness they showed toward me when they lived in safety in their land with no one to make them afraid.
Daniel 10:19	"Do not be afraid, O man highly esteemed," he said. "Peace! Be strong now; be strong." When he spoke to me, I was strengthened and said, "Speak, my lord, since you have given me strength."
Joel 2:21	Be not afraid, O land; be glad and rejoice. Surely the LORD has done great things.
Micah 4:4	Every man will sit under his own vine and under his own fig tree, and no one will make them afraid, for the LORD Almighty has spoken.
Zechariah 8:13	"As you have been an object of cursing among the nations, O Judah and Israel, so will I save you, and you will be a blessing. Do not be afraid, but let your hands be strong."
Zechariah 8:15	So now I have determined to do good again to Jerusalem and Judah. Do not be afraid.
Matthew 6:25	Therefore I tell you, do not worry about your life, what you will eat or drink; or about your body, what you will wear. Is not life more important than food, and the body more important than clothes?
Matthew 6:27	Who of you by worrying can add a single hour to his life?

Matthew 6:34	Therefore do not worry about tomorrow, for tomorrow will worry about itself. Each day has enough trouble of its own.
Matthew 8:26	He replied, "You of little faith, why are you so afraid?" Then he got up and rebuked the winds and the waves, and it was completely calm.
Matthew 10:31	So don't be afraid; you are worth more than many sparrows.
Matthew 14:27	But Jesus immediately said to them: "Take courage! It is I. Don't be afraid."
Matthew 14:30	But when he saw the wind, he was afraid and, beginning to sink, cried out, "Lord, save me!"
Matthew 17:7	But Jesus came and touched them. "Get up," he said. "Don't be afraid."
Matthew 28:10	Then Jesus said to them, "Do not be afraid. Go and tell my brothers to go to Galilee; there they will see me."
Mark 4:40	He said to his disciples, "Why are you so afraid? Do you still have no faith?"
Mark 5:36	Ignoring what they said, Jesus told the synagogue ruler, "Don't be afraid; just believe."
Mark 6:50	because they all saw him and were terrified. Immediately he spoke to them and said, "Take courage! It is I. Don't be afraid."
Luke 1:13	But the angel said to him: "Do not be afraid, Zechariah; your prayer has been heard. Your wife Elizabeth will bear you a son, and you are to give him the name John."
Luke 1:30	But the angel said to her, "Do not be afraid, Mary, you have found favor with God."
Luke 8:50	Hearing this, Jesus said to Jairus, "Don't be afraid; just believe, and she will be healed."
Luke 12:22	Then Jesus said to his disciples: "Therefore I tell you, do not worry about your life, what you will eat; or about your body, what you will wear."
Luke 12:25	Who of you by worrying can add a single hour to his life?
Luke 12:4	"I tell you, my friends, do not be afraid of those who kill the body and after that can do no more."

Luke 12:7	Indeed, the very hairs of your head are all numbered. Don't be afraid; you are worth more than many sparrows.
John 6:20	But he said to them, "It is I; don't be afraid."
John 12:15	"Do not be afraid, O Daughter of Zion; see, your king is coming, seated on a donkey's colt."
John 14:27	Peace I leave with you; my peace I give you. I do not give to you as the world gives. Do not let your hearts be troubled and do not be afraid.
Acts 18:9	One night the Lord spoke to Paul in a vision: "Do not be afraid; keep on speaking, do not be silent."
Romans 8:6	The mind of sinful man is death, but the mind controlled by the Spirit is life and peace . . .
Philippians 4:7	And the peace of God, which transcends all understanding, will guard your hearts and your minds in Christ Jesus.
Colossians 3:15	Let the peace of Christ rule in your hearts, since as members of one body you were called to peace. And be thankful.
2 Thessalonians 3:16	Now may the Lord of peace himself give you peace at all times and in every way. The Lord be with all of you.
2 Timothy 1:7	For God did not give us a spirit of timidity, but a spirit of power, of love and of self-discipline.
Hebrews 13:6	So we say with confidence, "The LORD is my helper; I will not be afraid. What can man do to me?"
Revelations 1:17	When I saw him, I fell at his feet as though dead. Then he placed his right hand on me and said: "Do not be afraid. I am the First and the Last."

ABOUT THE AUTHOR

Ashley and Jane Evans are senior pastors of Influencers Churches, a thriving apostolic movement with campuses in Australia, South Africa, and the United States. They are developing additional campuses in Malaysia and Papua-New Guinea. Together they host a television show that is broadcast worldwide six days a week.

In 2001, Ashley cofounded a political party in Australia called Family First. He has met numerous times with the prime minister and other senior ministers and currently mentors government leaders in public speaking.

Ashley is an innovative leader who has overcome many challenges in life to beat intimidation and fear. He has the unique ability to inspire the best in others and to create champions out of ordinary people. Known for his integrity and sincerity, Ashley is a gifted communicator whose greatest desire is to influence people for Christ.

Ashley and Jane currently reside in Atlanta, Georgia. They are the parents of three amazing sons: Mark, who is married to Lauren, Nathan, and Benjamin.

TO ORDER MORE COPIES

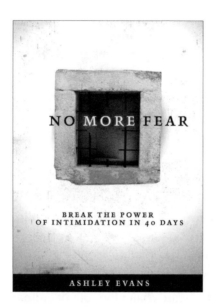

To order additional copies of
No More Fear, please visit
www.InfluenceResources.com.